My Dad, Our Alzheimer's: A Family's Spiritual Journey with the Other Side

Patricia Manly

My Dad Our Alzheimer's:
A Family's Spiritual Journey
with the Other Side

Copyright ©2014 by Patricia Manly
All rights reserved.

ISBN- 13:978-1499219227

Dedication

I dedicate this book to my mom, my best friend, my rock, my everything. I want to thank you for being there for me all those late nights and early mornings when I was scared and I thought I was going to collapse with exhaustion and you held me and told me that everything was going to be ok. I want to thank you for not giving up on Dad and staying as strong as you did when many would have given up. Without you, I would have never lasted the 5 years and 5 months that we took care of Dad with his journey with Alzheimer's. I love you forever.

Acknowledgements

I want to thank the following people in alphabetical order for being there for Dad, Mom and I before, during and after his passing. Whether it was directly or indirectly...All of you touched our hearts in so many ways. Each and every one of you gave us strength and love to keep us going strong through such a difficult time in our lives. With all of your love and support you made us feel like we existed in a time in our life when we needed you the most. God bless you all.

Joseph and CJ Allen
Amber Lynn Ashley
Janine Bennett
Kamara Best
Melissa Billups
David Burgess
Monica Burnett
LowandaRemy Butterfield,
LaMeisha Candler
Mr. and Mrs. Carrizosa
Tracy Casey
Terri Davault
Darlene Espinoza
Leslie Faamausili
Brenda Fleets
Leticia Flores
Kim Gomez
Paula Gore
Bridget Delph Gross
Daniel Guerry
Mel Hamilton
Rosalind Hamilton
Dondi Hawkins
Diane Linger Hill
Ellen Aitulani Seanoa Holani
Thomas R. Jackson
Aaron Keser
Nancy Lawson
Christopher & Amber Manly
Joseph Manly
Tammy Sprague Mann
Mike McRann

Darlene Miko
Tamra Morrison
Maira Nunez
Amanda Onofre
Francisco V Paras
Darcie Lynn Patino
Dore Perez
Mari Ramz
Ramona Roberts
DebraLynne Saavedra
Monica and Jessica Saenz
Martin Salazar
Rosie Sanchez
Jessyca Scott
Melle Rey-Shahabi
German Sierra
Bobby Sterling
Connie Sterling
Robert and Connie Sterling
Ronnie Sterling
Sara Minium- Stewart
Siri Traviglia
Cliff Truesdell
Lovey Tuinukuafe
Michael Valencia
Gary Vanderburg
La Nesa Wallace
Kim Pitts-Weber
LaShawn Westbrook
Tina and Jerry Whitcomb
Veronica Rey Winters
Bruce Wolfson

Contents

My Dad, Our Alzheimer's: A Family's Spiritual Journey with the Other Side	1
The Visitors	1
The Man He Used To Be	3
Three Days of Pain	7
The Three Warnings	10
Taking the Keys	13
The Road Trips	16
The Last Two Months	25
No More Suffering	53
The Visits	57
Dad's Message	68
I Remember When	71

The Visitors

In the five and a half years of taking care of Dad, the last two months have mentally and physically drained Mom and me more than ever before. Lying on the couch next to him and listening to him breathe, and the clock ticking away, feels so endless. I have slept next to him every night since Mom and I put him on hospice in September, but for some reason tonight the ticking of the clock sounds abnormally loud in my ears; as if it is letting me know the countdown has begun.

As he cried out all night because it was getting harder and harder for him to breathe as his lungs filled up with fluids, I would periodically tell him that I was there next to him, and that he was not alone. I sit up on the couch and watch him breathe. He takes deep breaths in and then stops breathing for a minute at a time between normal breaths. Then the whole cycle would start all over again. He has suffered so much on this journey, especially the last two months. It's too much for anyone to take. As I watch his chest rise and fall and then stop all together, I wonder how much longer he can go on like this.

I get off the couch; sleep isn't going to happen just yet. I lay next to Dad. I needed to hear his heartbeat. I just have this feeling that it isn't going to be much longer before it was going to stop beating forever. I put my ear to his chest. His heart sounded so faint. The fluids filling up in his lungs drowned what I was so desperately trying to hear. Between sobs I tell Dad that he was everything I wished and prayed for in a Father. I tell him that he has given me so much joy, so much endless love. I tell him that he doesn't have to worry; I will keep my promise and take care of Mom just like I took care of him. I tell him that it is time to let go; Mom and I would be ok. He doesn't have to hold on anymore; it is time to go home now.

Even though I did not want Dad to leave us or even admit that his life here on earth was coming to an end, I did not want him to suffer one more day. I can't take it anymore. I try to lay with him as long as possible, but the sounds of his lungs filling are torturing my mind, especially since I can't do anything for him. Every second, every minute, of hearing the wet crackling sounds of his lungs, feels like an eternity. I get up, stroke his hair, kiss his forehead, and once again let him know that I am right next to him on the couch.

Early in the morning, something woke me up. I look over at Dad as I always do when I hear him stir or make a noise. What I saw made my heart drop. In the light glow of the kitchen nightlight, I saw two men dressed in dark suits sitting next to Dad as he lay in his bed. The men were in solid form but looked like they were from another dimension. In front of them was a wall of ripples or wavy lines that went from floor to ceiling; like a mirage on hot pavement. When I saw them I felt no fear. Though I could not hear them, I could see their mouths moving in conversation. The man nearest Dad's head had a thin build with strong pointy features and wore a hat. The other man looked younger and stockier. Both men appeared to be dressed in clothing from the early 1900's. I have heard many stories of how our loved ones or Angels come to us right before our demise to help us transition over to the other side. I knew they had come for him. Shocked, all I could do was stare at them. They looked at me for just a moment then they got up and slowly walked- or I should say, floated – away, with Dad, through the wall in the dining area. Frantically, I looked back at the bed and saw Dad, still there, breathing shallow, his lungs still making those horrible wet crackling sounds. I knew then that my best friend, my Dad, was going home soon.

After Dad passed, I was looking through old pictures and I saw these two men. One of them was definitely Mr. Ovitt, the man who took Dad in when he was 12 years old, and the other man looked a lot like Charlie, Dad's brother.

The Man He Used To Be

Everyone has a story. Even though Dad could not share it when he was here on this earth, he deserves to have his personal story told. Dad's story needs to be explained to the many who only knew the man he was before Alzheimer's set in. Dad endured such pain and misery at such a young age that I truly believe it molded him to be the angry man he was the majority of his life. I am not making excuses for him, but for me personally, I now understand the man that we used to know most of our lives. This is his story.

George Rodney Manly (Dad) was born in Boston, Massachusetts, on February 02, 1929 to parents of Irish and German descent. They were both from New York City. He was the youngest of six children; four sisters and one brother.

On a visit to see his sister Katherine in Florida in 2009, Dad and his sister told Mom and me exactly what happened in their childhood. I don't want to get in too deep on specific details of how his dad inflicted terror on his family, but I will say this much: there was extreme mental, verbal, and physical abuse. On many occasions it took place in the basement of their house. In addition, their father attempted suicide right in front of them, so often that his mom carried scissors in her house dress in case he needed to be cut down again.

I began to fully understand the emotional affects this had on Dad until a week before he died. I was sitting next to Dad as he was lying in his hospice bed telling him it was almost time for him to go home.

"Dad, when God comes for you, you're going to see your mom again." "Yes." he replied with a peaceful smile on his face. "And your sister Elizabeth." "Yes.". "And Charlie." "Yes". If I would have known how the next statement affected him, I would have never said it. I then said to him, "And you're going to see your Dad too." His eyes got really wide and I saw fear in them. He pulled up his blanket so fast to his chin and said "No, no, I don't want to see him!" I held his hand and I said, "Ok, Dad, I am sorry. I didn't mean to say your dad, ok? You won't see your dad." He relaxed and said, "Ok good, because I don't want to see him, ok? I don't want to ever see him." I never mentioned his dad again in our conversations.

As Dad got older, his childhood changed for the better. In 1941, at 12-years-old Dad was sent to work on a farm in Vermont. The couple took him in and treated him as one of their own. Mr. and Mrs. Ovitt gave him his own room and his first 22 rifle (which to this day is in a safe place with bullets still in their box from his childhood).

He stayed with Mr. and Mrs. Ovitt until he was 19 years old. The long hard hours on the farm instilled in him the work ethic he carried throughout his life, and passed on to his children.

While Dad was on the Ovitt's farm, he found a love for weightlifting. He once told me how he made his first weights by attaching two metal milk buckets filled with cement, to a plow bar with two chains connecting the buckets together. He used his homemade weights for deadlifts, bench presses, and squats. In 1983, 35 years later, Dad took us to the Ovitt farm. To Dad's surprise, Mrs. Ovitt kept those make shift weights in the barn where he last left them as a kid. When we left, she gave them to him to bring home. Dad was so happy. You could see on his face that those weights brought back so many good memories.

Whatever job Dad had, it always had to do with boats, ships and the ocean. He was in his 20's when he started working on a tugboat on the docks in New York City. He then worked for the United Fruit Company transporting bananas from Costa Rica to the United States. During the Vietnam War, he was a Merchant Mariner with the Coast Guard carrying supplies back and forth through the Panama Canal to our Men and Women in uniform. His last job was as a Chief Engineer for Mobil Oil Corporation. He worked for Mobil Oil for 16 years, till he retired at the age of 67 in 1993.

Mom and Dad met in 1962 on a freighter going to Jamaica and Honduras. Mom was on vacation and Dad worked on the Freighter that Mom was vacationing on. Since Mom was by herself, she decided to take herself on a little tour on the ship. She didn't know she was in a restricted area until Dad came along. His first words to her were, "You know you are not supposed to be in this area." Later that same night he asked her out to dinner. Mom said that Dad was very funny and had her laughing as he made jokes all night. She loved this about him. They ate dinner and later danced. Mom said Dad was totally flirting with her all night, and that he danced really well. They ended the night by Dad walking Mom back to her room and gave her a kiss on the lips. They decided to go to breakfast together the next morning. After Breakfast and a swim in the pool at the Hilton, they left to go back to the ship. The streets were filled with people celebrating their independence from England that was won the day before they came into shore, so they walked back to the ship instead of getting a cab. On the last day of the cruise, Dad told mom he wanted to see her again and to get the ship's paper because there was something in there he wanted her to see. The Ship's newspaper had an article about Mom and Dad's shipboard romance. Dad had personally put this in the paper to impress her. As the ship made it back to New York Harbor, Dad approached Mom and said he would like to make plans to see her again. Two months later they got married on June 15th 1963.

In July 1966, they moved to California and had six children together. In 1974, Dad became a different person. Why, I don't think anyone will ever know. It seemed like he changed overnight. Dad became a very angry man. He instilled fear both mentally and physically for most of our childhood. Mom told me that it may have been when they were looking at a house which they eventually bought against Moms wishes. Right before she entered the house, she heard a man's voice say to her "You will never be happy here!". To this day Mom says she wished she would have listened; maybe, just maybe things would have been better for all of us.

But between the abuses, he showed his love with vacations around the country. Even though these vacations could never make up for what happened inside our four walls, these trips left us with many good memories of him to cherish forever. Dad always loved us, even though he couldn't show it or say it the way we would have loved him to. I personally believe he hated who he was. I know this to be true because of the conversation he and I had just one month before his passing.

We sat outside the house together. Dad looked very solemn and was very quiet. I asked him if he was ok. He was looking down at his clasped hands and shaking his head slowly back and forth. I asked him again what was wrong. He continued looking down, almost like he was ashamed of himself, and said, "I feel so bad." I asked him what he meant by that. He said "I just feel so bad. I hurt so many people. I was such a mean, angry man". I said "What do you mean Dad? Who did you hurt?" He said, "Everyone. I hurt so many people, all of my kids, my wife, and I feel so bad." I saw tears flowing from his eyes. I got up and sat next to him and I said, "Dad, you are not that man anymore. You are a good guy now." He shrugged and continued to say, "I just feel so bad."

I said, "Let it go Dad, it's the past, it's over with. You are not that man anymore. You are not the man you used to be". He shrugged and continued to slowly shake his head back and forth. I could see the pain and guilt in his eyes. No matter what I said, there was no convincing him. After that day, Dad never spoke of this again.

Dad started professional powerlifting in 1977. He received many world and national titles. To this day, no one can beat two of his titles. In 2007 at the age of 76, he had to give up on his lifelong love of powerlifting because Alzheimer's was setting in. He was devastated. I found him crying hard in the shed one day in 2008, as he was looking at his medals, trophies, and pictures of himself weightlifting. I told him that he was one of the most amazing weightlifters ever, and that he had so many trophies and medals to show for it. I also told him that every weightlifter would have to face the same choice that he had to make. I said to him, "Dad, you powerlifted for many years. It's time for you to give your body a rest now, just like it was time for you to retire from your job." He nodded and said in between crying, "I miss my shipmates too. I miss going to the tournaments. I miss everything I used to do." There was nothing I could say or do to fill the emptiness or loss that he was feeling. I stood there next to him and watched him silently as the tears continued to flow.

Three Days of Pain

July 2007

This is really where Dad's journey with Alzheimer's begins. From this day forward, our lives changed forever. I believe that everything that happened and the way he developed Alzheimer's was to humble him to make him the man he needed to be to get where he is now. I truly believe that he would have never changed into the beautiful man that he became unless he developed Alzheimer's.

Mom and I noticed Dad to be acting differently, very quiet and into himself. Mom asked him if he was ok, and he told us he wasn't feeling too well. He went and laid down for a nap. It is very rare that he gets sick. Last time he was sick was when he had prostate cancer in 2000.

For the next two days he stayed in his room. Mom and I periodically checked in on him, but he told us every time that all he needed was sleep and to leave him alone. On the third morning, Mom and I agreed that this had gone on too long. I went to his room, turned the knob, and found it was locked. I knocked on the door and he did not answer. I knocked again, no answer. I went to my bathroom and got a Q-tip, came back and turned on the hall light. I inserted the Q-tip in the hole of the door knob as I had done so many times as a kid when a door was locked on purpose. I opened the door. His room was somewhat dark. From the light in the hallway, I could make out his form lying on the bed. He was facing the wall. I called him and he turned toward me. He was very angry and told me to get the hell out. I let him know that he didn't answer the door when I knocked, so I got worried and had to check in on him and make sure he was ok. Dad told me he felt like he had the flu and he just needed his sleep. I stood there for a minute contemplating whether I should ask him to at least eat some soup, but I knew it would have upset him even more. What Dad says goes. So I let him know that there was water and crackers on the dresser if he should get hungry.

Early that evening I went to his room to check in on him. I heard him talking. I stood outside his door listening. I heard him cry out, "Oh my God it hurts! Oh man it hurts so bad!" I asked him to please let me help him, but he yelled at me to go away. I said, "Dad, this is not normal for you, open the door! Let me take you to the hospital, please!" He said, "Just leave me alone, I just want to sleep!" I said, "Dad just let me check you out and I promise I will leave you alone."

I heard him moving around in his room and then I heard him unlock the door. He didn't look good. He looked like he was in pain and very pale. I asked him what his symptoms were. He told me his mouth hurt really badly and the pain went into his head. I asked once again to let me take him to the hospital just to get checked out, or at least let me take him to the doctor. Mom said, "George, let Patricia take you to the hospital, please!" Dad said, "No! I don't want to go to the hospital or the doctor! I will get better. Don't worry about it, now leave me alone! I just want to sleep!" I thought maybe he had a cavity that's affecting his root. The only thing that I could think of until he gave in to going to the doctor was to give him some chelation mouth wash and vitamin C in case he had an infection. He let me give him the mouth wash and vitamin C and then he went back to bed, once again telling me to leave him alone and just let him sleep.

After trying to convince him to go to the hospital, I sat down with Mom and we decided this would be the last night Dad would lock himself in his room; we would make an appointment with the doctor for tomorrow whether he wanted to go or not. I kissed Mom goodnight and headed to the bathroom.

I had just gotten out of the shower and I looked down the hallway to Dad's room, and what I saw stopped me in my tracks...

There were so many of them.

Huge, tall men wearing black suits, appeared out of nowhere in the middle of the living room and walked fast towards Dads room. They were about 7 feet tall, white-greyish skin with big bulky heads and they literally looked like they had just risen from the grave. There was a white-grey mist around them and as they walked towards Dad's room, the mist followed them. These men or things or whatever they were, were literally piling into Dad's room. It was almost animated watching these things because in reality so many would have never been able to go in at one time through the bedroom door as they did. They were piling in so fast that it looked like they were each trying to get to whatever they were going first, before the others. After watching the last one go in Dad's room, I stood there for a moment and listened. I slowly walked toward Dad's room. I blessed myself with holy water. I got to the hallway and stopped. I noticed the bedroom door wide open and I called out to Dad. No answer. I nervously cleared my throat and called out to Dad again. He angrily answered this time "What!" I entered his room; it felt so eerie and somewhat cold. I looked around and didn't see anything of what I just saw a few moments ago.

I said, "Are you ok Dad?" Dad said, "Yeah, what do you want!? I told you I didn't want you bothering me!" I said, "I heard a noise and I noticed your door was open, so I thought I would check in on you. Are you feeling any better?" He said, "A little. I'm just tired and my mouth hurts." I asked him if he was hungry and he told me he was a little hungry, so I made him some chicken noodle soup. I sat with him at the table. I watched him eat for some time before I asked him if he heard any noises in his room before I came in. He was silent for a minute, deep in thought, looking down at his food. Then he said, "I had a nightmare." I asked what it was about and he told me it didn't matter, that it was just a nightmare and that he had been having them for the past three nights.

The Three Warnings

July 2007

The next three nights after Dad locked himself in his room, he came to me telling me that a man kept coming to him and waking him up. On the third night it was about 11:30 when Dad entered my room. He was visibly upset. He told me that this man who keeps coming to him is being persistent and won't leave him alone. He told me that this man continues to tell him that he better change before it's too late. I told him he was probably just having a bad dream. I really didn't know what else to say because I had never heard him speak this way or act this worried about some man coming to him. He continued to stand there looking to me for answers to why this was happening to him, and all I could do was look back at him. I was at a loss for words of why this was happening.

He finally said, "You know what I told him Patreesha!?" I said, "What did you tell him?" He said, "I told him I ain't changing for nobody!" I looked into Dad's eyes. I not only saw anger but I also saw worry and fear. I said, "You don't think you should listen, Dad?" He said, "Nope, like I said, I am not changing for nobody!"

I felt such sadness for him. Three days of pain and now this man who kept coming to Dad telling him he better change. Something didn't feel right with all of this. I was trying to put all this together, but nothing made sense. I didn't have any answers for Dad. I told him that maybe he needed to listen to this man who kept coming to him. Maybe there was a reason for this message. He looked at me and said in a tired voice, "Well, like I said, I am not changing for no one." All I could do was just look at him. What else could I tell him? He's someone you can't tell what to do, especially when his mind is set.

The next morning I woke up and went to the kitchen and stopped because I thought I heard crying. As I stood there I heard it again. The crying was coming from Dad's room. As I approached his door, I heard crying that was so deeply troubling and sounded so intense, so lost. I stood there at the door and listened to a man who rarely showed any emotions besides anger, crying like I have never heard him cry before. As I think back, the only other time I heard him cry was when Mom went into the hospital for chest pain and Dad thought he was going to lose her. I opened the door and I found him standing in the dark in the middle of his room crying. I turned the light on. He was holding the remote to the TV in his hand saying, "I'm trying to turn it on but there is nothing there!" Over and over he would repeat these same words in between sobbing. So I went over to the T.V and turned it on. I said, "Dad it works, I got it on for you."

He continued to look at the T.V. remote and look back at me and say, "No you don't understand, I am trying to turn it on, but there is nothing there, it's empty, it's all empty, there is nothing there, it's empty!" I stood there looking at Dad and it finally hit me. He was telling me he could no longer think and that his mind was empty. He took my hand and in between his sobbing and crying he continued to tell me while he hit his head in frustration with the TV remote, that there was nothing there, that it was empty. I grabbed the remote and took it away from him. He said, "Please help me, help me, there is nothing there! Help me please! I don't know what to do!" I held him and he held me so hard. I felt him shaking. He was so scared and for the first time this once strong man was asking me to help him and all I could think was, "God please help me help my Dad." To this day I wonder, what if he wouldn't have denied that Man's three warnings to change. Would his journey have been different? Would he still have developed Alzheimer's?

From that day on we went to both holistic and conventional doctors seeking the best treatment for Dad's Alzheimer's. Blood work was taken, CT scans etc., with the exception of the elevated inflammation levels, all of Dads test came back normal. Dad was put on a chelation detox program right away because the holistic doctor thought that he had exposure to mercury from his fillings in his teeth. Later that week the dentist told us that Dad does not have nearly enough metal in his mouth to cause the symptoms he suffered with. He said that there is only one tooth that has mercury in it is still intact with no leakage. I don't think we will ever know what happened to cause Dad's three days of pain and extreme memory loss.

Within about a week of the holistic doctor's detox treatment, we noticed a marked improvement with his mental status. We had to reteach him how to work the T.V. and the computer, and show him where everything was in the house. Slowly he was getting back his ability to do things on his own again, even drive.

Taking the Keys

September 2007

To take the keys away from a man that you have known to be one of the strongest people in your life humbles you in so many ways. Seeing my dad's eyes everything that ever made him a "man" was slowly being taken away from him one by one, is one of the saddest experiences of my life.

Mom came to my room and woke me up to tell me that Dad was on the phone and he lost his keys. As I answered the phone, Dad proceeded to tell me he lost his keys somewhere in the store and asked me to bring him the spare. As I pulled up to him in the parking lot, he appeared embarrassed and lost standing next to his car with his arms crossed. I got out and gave him the keys. He told me in an uncertain voice about how weird it was that his keys just disappeared. I told him to not worry about it because I have also misplaced my keys before. I kissed him goodbye and got back in my car and drove away. As I looked in my rear view mirror, I saw him on his hands and knees, looking under his car, maybe trying one last time to find his keys.

After I got back from taking him the keys, Mom told me more. She said that when driving, at times he would just come to a stop in the middle of an intersection and just sit there with a blank look on his face until she would tell him that he needs to get moving out of the intersection. She also told me that Dad's driving was becoming erratic. Along with backing into poles and going through red lights, he was also becoming more aggressive toward other drivers.

Over the next few weeks I noticed more and more damage to Dad's car. When he came home with half of the front bumper to his car hanging off, I knew I had to take action. I had to take the keys once and for all, not only to protect the public but to protect him. It hurt me deeply to convince him that something he had done since a teenager, the one last thing that made him feel independent, was going to be taken from him. Now I just had to think of something that would convince him to hand over the keys without an argument or make him feel like he couldn't do anything on his own anymore. What we came up with luckily convinced Dad that handing over the keys would be the best thing for the time being. I told him that since his doctor had him detoxing metals and toxins from his body, that there was a big chance that he could pass out at the wheel. And if that happened the DMV would take his license away because he would now be considered not only a danger to himself, but to the public. He was upset but he reluctantly handed me the keys. I let him know that it was just for now, just till his body healed.

The next day I woke up from a nap and found him gone. My heart dropped. I looked outside and saw that the car was gone. I didn't even think to get the spare key from him. Later on I found an additional five sets in different places in his room. I sat on the couch and prayed the whole time. I waited for him to come back, hoping and praying he wouldn't hurt himself or someone else. I heard the front door open and I watched him come in with a bag of groceries and a huge smile on his face. I asked, "Where were you!? Why did you leave!? You're not supposed to leave Dad; you're not supposed to drive!" I was so upset because he literally could have killed himself or someone else. He ignored me, continued to the kitchen, and put the grocery bag on the counter. He pulled out a lemon cake and said, "Let's celebrate! I made it home! I told you I can make it home! I found my way back home! Let's celebrate!"

I couldn't even respond. What he said brought instant tears. He knew he was losing his mind and all I could do was sit there and cry for him. I wanted to just hold him and tell him that his mind would be ok, but all I could think of was how sad it was to think of what was going on inside his mind, and to feel what he was feeling right then and there. How scary it must be to know that your mind is slowly dying. That one day you will not remember your loved ones, or where you are, and worse yet, no longer knowing yourself.

I said, "Dad we need to talk. Please come here and sit down." He came over to the couch and sat down next to me. I said, "I am happy you made it home, but you can't do this anymore. You can't leave and drive the car. Please Dad, just until you are done with your detox, no more driving ok?" He said, "I just don't understand why. I made it home. I proved that I can make it home. Why can't I drive?" I said, "A few more weeks, ok? Just a few more weeks." He said, "Will you take me everywhere I need to go?" I said, "Yes Dad, I will be your personal chauffer." He said, "Ok, just a few weeks and then I can go back to driving. Now let's have some cake!"

Eventually as time went on, and with me telling Dad just a few more weeks each time he asked, he no longer asked to drive. His Alzheimer's had progressed to a point where he was no longer confident in driving. At the time I thought I was losing my Dad to a horrific disease. But little did I know I was going to be blessed with everything I did not get as a little girl, everything that I wished and prayed for in a dad.

The Road Trips

2009 Road Trip

Between 2009 and 2011, Mom, Dad and I went on two road trips. The first one consisted of driving 10,000 miles in 23 days through 32 states. We went around the U.S and visited family and friends, some of them for the first time. Mom and I also had a surprise for Dad with a visit to his two sisters whom he hadn't seen in over 40 years. As I had never met them either, this was very exciting for me as well.

We learned really quickly that Dad couldn't stay in one place for long periods at a time. We visited Mom and Dad's grandkids in South Carolina, my nieces and nephews Miguel and Stephanie and their kids MJ and Eleyna. Even though this was the first time meeting them, they welcomed us with open arms into their home, as if they have known us forever. We took pictures and had a really good BBQ for lunch together, and before we departed we made sure that we would keep in touch.

Our next stop was to Florida to visit Dad's sister Katherine. She also had Alzheimer's; as a matter of fact, five out of Dad's six siblings developed Alzheimer's. The sixth one, Dad's only brother Charlie, died of cirrhosis of the liver. Aunt Katherine said that Charlie was showing signs of Alzheimer's as well, but died before he was diagnosed. When we pulled up in Aunt Katherine's driveway, she was waiting for us with a big smile on her face. You could tell that Dad and Aunt Katherine were brother and sister; they looked so much alike. Before we got out of the car, Dad just stared at Aunt Katherine and said, "That's my sister, isn't it?" I said, "Yes, that's Katherine." Dad got out of the car and they both just stared at each other. Aunt Katherine said, "Your my baby brother, George" and Dad said, "And you're my sister." Aunt Katherine and Dad hugged, joked, and laughed while introducing me for the first time. Cousin Pat, who I also met for the first time, came by and we all set out to go have lunch at a restaurant on the beach. Good food, great drinks, and good times. I couldn't stop staring at Aunt Katherine and Dad, they looked truly happy. They sat right next to each other and just enjoyed the moment. For the first time on the trip, Dad was actually relaxed and enjoying every moment with his sister. That night, Aunt Katherine insisted we stay the night at her house, but we told her it wasn't a good idea because Dad wanders the house throughout the night. Still, she insisted that I sleep in her room with her and Mom and Dad sleep in the guest room.

That night Aunt Katherine and I talked for hours about everything, including their childhood growing up. I heard many horrific stories of just how brutal Dad's dad was to all of them. After Aunt Katherine went into detail of exactly what happened in their house growing up, especially the basement, I had a better understanding of why Dad was who he was the majority of his life, and why he was such an angry man. Early in the morning, about 3:00 a.m., I heard movement outside Aunt Katherine's room in the hallway; as usual, Dad was making his rounds, of course, in only his underwear. One by one, I would hear a click as he turned on every light in the house. I helped him back to his room and put him back to bed, hoping I would at least get another hour of sleep before he made another round.

Later that morning we had a wonderful breakfast out in the screen room. We talked some more about the good times and how we should all keep in touch and visit again in the near future. We looked at many photo albums and Aunt Katherine gave us photos to bring back with us. Little did I know that that visit with Aunt Katherine would be the last; she passed away in 2013, just 6 months after Dad. I was so happy to meet such a beautiful soul before she passed.

Our next stop was to Georgia to visit my half-brother George (Dad's son from another marriage) his wife Terry, and their only daughter Irina. They also welcomed us into their home with open and compassionate arms. Even though the visit was short we had an awesome time together. They were beautiful people I was finally able to meet for the first time in my life.

After leaving George and Terry's house we headed on over to New Jersey to meet with my niece Drea, Mom and Dad's granddaughter, for the first time. What a beautiful young lady, both inside and out. Drea took us on a scenic drive and showed us around her neighborhood. We ate lunch together and like the other visits, this one was also short due to Dad's anxiety. But the time that we spent together was amazing and one we will never forget.

We left later to a hotel in Ohio to get some rest before we headed out the next morning to Michigan. On the way to Ohio, we went through practically every east coast state. Mom wanted to visit her parents' gravesite in New York. By the time we made it to New York, Dad's anxiety kicked in, so stopping in Queens to visit Mom's parents' gravesite was not going to happen on this visit. We kept going, stopping only for gas and food. We made it to a small hotel in Ohio and called it a night.

We headed out the next morning and a few hours later we finally pulled into my brother's driveway, where Joe, my sister -in- law Cristina, my niece Kaehla, and my nephew Noah were waiting to greet us. Many tears were shed on this visit, balanced by the laughter and good times we had together. We stayed the night and left the next morning.

The next stop was Indiana to visit my Dad's other sister, Elizabeth in a convalescent home. When we pulled up, she was not only sitting outside with her son Roger, and his wife; unbeknownst to us, it was her birthday. We visited for a few hours and once again laughed and made so many good memories together. Two weeks later after visiting for the first time in 40 years, Aunt Elizabeth passed away in her sleep. We were very blessed to be able to visit before she passed. I will never forget the way they looked at each other on that very memorable visit. I didn't think with their Alzheimer's that they would remember each other, but they did, and that's all that mattered on this trip. None of us will ever forget the memories we made on that trip.

2011 Road Trip

Our second road trip that Mom and I decided to take was for Thanksgiving to see my nephew Christopher and family in Colorado. I was actually very nervous and excited at the same time. Nervous, because I didn't know how Dad was going to handle it, and excited because we were going to see family for Thanksgiving. I went to the doctors with Dad to get some type of medicine to help him relax on the trip. The doctor gave us some Xanax. I journaled every day of this trip. I wanted to remember every detail because I had a feeling that this would be Dad's last trip with us all together.

20 November

Mom, Dad and I are leaving in less than an hour. We are taking a little road trip. We are going to be driving 17 hours, 1500 miles one way, about 3000 round trip, starting today. I am a little scared because I don't know how Dad is going to react on this trip. We are going to celebrate Thanksgiving with my nephew Christopher, my niece Amber, and my great nieces Alayna and Kiahna.

20 November

I just drove 400 miles in 7 hours today. I had to stop because Dad was getting anxious. The only reason I drove so many miles today is because I needed to get as far as possible so we could relax the rest of the days on this trip for Dad. Going for long periods I notice it does a lot to him mentally. So we got a hotel room. Before we call it a night I am going to take Dad for a little walk; maybe this will help his anxiety and help him sleep better. I feel so bad. I want to turn around because I don't want Dad to feel this way. But when we were at home, he felt the same way, anxious. I just need to remember that making memories is very important and staying at home would be just a waste of some beautiful moments to be made.

21 November

I was going to turn around and go home today. Last night was a bad night with Dad. He started to hallucinate and attempt on multiple occasions to get outside the hotel room. He wet the bed and could not relax at all.

All of this was just too much to take on. I was up all night with Dad. I told Mom, "Dad is hallucinating and he is reaching for things that are not even there." He asked on multiple occasions about the voices. I felt so guilty, if I went home all we would do is sit behind 4 walls and not celebrate Thanksgiving, or we could continue to deal with the extreme stress of Dad's declining mental status and hopefully have a wonderful time at Thanksgiving with family. I did not want to hurt Dad in anyway and I was trying to make the best decision. If we went home Dad would continue with multiple episodes of roaming the house and opening and closing the doors. Mom said we should keep going, either way Dad would be Dad because of his Alzheimer's.

As for now Mom and I have decided to continue on with the trip to Colorado and head to New Mexico and stay overnight in another hotel. We will travel about 350 miles today.

I am scared but I have to do this. This trip means so many things, not just for me, but the beautiful memories we will share and make that we might not get to make next year. This is why I am pushing so hard. We all deserve this. Nothing is worth passing up beautiful moments that we are going to make together. Mom and Dad will see their two great granddaughters for the first time, seeing Lil Chris and Amber and brother Joe, and that's what keeps me pushing through - memories. When it is all said and done no matter what happens on this trip, there will be memories made that each of us will cherish forever.

22 November

I did another 500 miles again. I was only supposed to do 350 miles, but we did not like the area we were in, so we continued on into northern New Mexico. We are about four hours from family.

Dad has not slept at all. He is getting so anxious I do not know what to do. Mom and I have not slept at all either. I gave Dad some medicine that the doctor gave to him for the trip, but so far it hasn't helped at all. He is talking incoherently and he is saying there are people outside.

I want to cry. Mom and I need our sleep so bad. I feel sad for Dad because he cannot control what he is doing. Dad is going on almost 48 hours of no sleep along with Mom and me. Two more days till Thanksgiving and I do not know how much worse it will get with him.

We've come too far to turn around now. Dad does not know who we are at all; he thinks we are his shipmates. I can't stop crying. It feels like I am losing him so fast. He is starting to get aggressive. He put his fist up to me when I was guiding him back to bed, and he pushed Mom aside to get outside. I cannot believe how close I was to calling the cops, that is how aggressive and uncontrollable Dad became. If I would have stayed at home, Dad wouldn't be this bad. I am thinking it is my fault. Dad is now not listening to us. I cannot believe what this trip has done to him. Two days till Thanksgiving and I am praying Dad does not get worse before then.

23 November

We got into town where Lil Chris lives and checked into the hotel. Early in the evening, Dad's symptoms became even more bizarre. I noticed his left pupil was slightly larger. Dad did not look like Dad. He had this glazed look in his eyes. His speech became impaired and stuttered, and his words became mumbles. We took him to the hospital where he was immediately admitted.

I was sitting next to his hospital bed and he said to me, "My mom and brother have been visiting me for the past two days." (Both are deceased). The nurse let us know that Dad will be having more lab work, X-ray, MRI and echocardiogram.

As of right now, he cannot walk on his own and he has left-sided weakness. The nurse also said if they do not find anything, that most likely he will be released tomorrow if everything comes back normal. I hope we can all spend Thanksgiving together.

I really don't know how my mind and body can handle all of this stress, let alone Mom. I feel sometimes I am going to break at the seams. I just have to keep thinking that this Thanksgiving with family will all be worth it.

24 November

I got back late last night. I visited with dad. I wish I could have stayed there overnight with him, but they had no bed and I so desperately needed sleep. He is doing very well. The day before yesterday, he couldn't stand on his own or walk or use his left hand. At this time they have him sedated with Haldol.

Yesterday he stood up by himself and can now walk with one person. When eating, he uses a fork in his right hand and the knife in his left hand. He has equal grips now along with no more of a wild glazed look. He also has his awesome sense of humor back. Last night they did not know when he would be discharged. They have him on Haldol and he is getting the sleep he so desperately needs.

I called the hospital about 30 minutes ago and Dad will be released for Thanksgiving. Everyone is so happy to hear that he will be discharged. We are going to enjoy such a beautiful day with our beautiful family.

25 November

We are on our way to the hospital to pick up Dad. It is Thanksgiving and we are really looking forward to getting him out of the hospital and coming home and eating as much as he wants.

Mom and I are somewhat uncertain if everything is going to be ok with him coming out of the hospital, but this is what we came all this way for. We entered the hospital very anxious but excited to finally see Dad. As we were turning the corner to the hallway where his room is, I saw a man standing halfway out of the room peeking down the hallway toward our way.

I kept looking and I wasn't sure if it was Dad because, number one, he was too far away and two, Dad wasn't able to stand on his own by himself when I had last seen him yesterday.

As I was getting closer, I said out loud to mom, "Is that Dad!?" Dad looked at me and said out loud, "That's my daughter right there!" I got tears in my eyes. I was so happy to see him. I finally reached him and held and kissed his cheeks.

I asked if he knew who I was, and to my surprise he said, "You're my daughter Patreesha!" He knew who I was and he was standing on his own! He went to Mom and held both her hands and said, "There's my Mama" and gave her a kiss on her lips. Dad is not 100% the way he was when we left for the trip, but we got the majority of him back, and I will take that any day.

Thanksgiving was awesome and Dad had two plates of everything and two pieces of pie. Afterwards we all relaxed for the rest of the day. We laughed about everything and had such a good time. We were in good company. No stress, just laughing and talking and playing with the babies.

26 November

My brother Joe came into town the next day. We all went to the Garden of the Gods and it was packed. It was a winding road up the mountains. The beauty of the red rock formations was just amazing. Dad was surprisingly doing really well. We stopped and walked for a while and before we left, we took many pictures.

After our outing at Garden of the Gods, we picked up dinner and went back to the house. We had such a good time and it felt so good to sit with family and actually enjoy each other's company. I really do not want this to end. I want to have these get-togethers forever, but I know soon we will have to go back home again.

Today was also a sad day, especially for my brother. Joe asked Dad if he knew who he was, and Dad just looked away, because he didn't know who he was. Joe cried hard. I could see the pain in his eyes. I felt so sorry for him. I remember how I felt when Dad said he didn't know who I was the first time. To have one of your parents not know who you are is one of the most painful things one can go through in one's lifetime.

I left to go to the pharmacy for Dad's medicine, and Joe told me when I came back that Dad cried when I left and asked where I was. Joe told Dad that I would be back soon.

When I came back, Joe said that Dad stood by the window the whole time I was gone waiting for me to come back, and that he smiled and said, "There she is!" when he saw me pulling up. He greeted me at the door with a huge smile.

Dad asked to take a nap, so I brought him back to one of the empty rooms, and he stared at the ceiling as he lay in the bed. I asked him if he was ok, and he told me he didn't know. I asked if he was depressed and he told me no. I then asked him if he was sad and he said "yes." I asked him why and he told me because he couldn't just walk out of the house anymore and do the things he used to do. I said, "Yes you can, you can do whatever you want. The only difference is that I will be right by your side doing it with you." He got tears in his eyes, looked at me and said, "Thank you for not leaving me alone, I would be lost without you." I told him I will never leave him.

We are going to have a big homemade breakfast tomorrow morning before Joe leaves to go back home, and end the day with an early dinner before Lil Chris takes Joe to the airport. I wish this didn't have to end and we all lived closer. Joe brought up that it would be nice if we could all live near each other, and how many get-togethers we could have. That would be so nice. I know Mom would love it. If it wasn't for the cold, I would be there in a second just to be near family.

Tonight I gave Dad his first dose of Haldol. I hope it works. He needs his sleep and so do we.

27 November

Today is the day we head back home, but before we left Dad had us all in tears just by what he had to say to us. Mom, Dad and I were sitting in the car and Joe, Lil Chris and Amber and his kids were standing next to Dad's open door when he started to speak. He sounded so clear of mind when saying what he said to us.

He told Joe and Chris to always love their family first and they will love him for that. He said, "When it is time I will see Jesus along the way to heaven, and one day we will all be together again." He looked at Chris and Amber and said, "Love and cherish your family, because in the end that is all you have." No one had a dry eye. Dad spoke so clearly, with no hesitation. It was truly amazing.

28 November

We just got back into our home town and shockingly I am actually happy to be back. This last leg of the trip, I had difficult challenges. I drove 800 miles today. Dad was so anxious and he was begging me to get home now; don't stop. Even though I was tired I kept going because I did not want anything else to happen with him.

He is doing a lot better now that he is back at home. At first when we got inside the house, he didn't recognize his surroundings. But after about an hour he knew where he was. I put him to bed and Mom and I sat down to talk.

I said to Mom, "Did you have a good time, was it worth it?" She said, "Putting the hotel and hospital situation aside, it is always worth it when you are making memories with the people who love you."

The Last Two Months

The last two months of Dad's life will be embedded in me and Mom's minds forever. From September 5th till November 7th, Dad's journey took us on a rollercoaster ride of extreme emotional highs and lows. Watching him stop breathing in front of us six times almost broke us, and not being able to do anything to save him was an endless nightmare. To watch someone you have grown to love more than yourself take his last breath over and over again will break even the strongest person. This is what Mom, Dad and I endured on a daily basis. These next two months went from hopeful to hopeless over and over again until Dad took his last breath. I journaled almost every day of the last two months of Dad's life.

September 2012

Dad is becoming nonstop. He needs to see us at all times even to the point of following us to the bathroom. He has aged so much just in the past three months. He is getting that faraway look and losing some of his sense of humor.

I made myself numb for a while now. I don't really want to face what's to come. I have to hold his hand everywhere we go. He is scared about everything, especially when I am not around. I am tired. Mentally and physically Mom and I are really tired.

I want Dad to live forever but I know that is so selfish of me. He is suffering. If I were in his shoes, I wouldn't want to be around for even a minute not knowing who my loved ones are, not being able to dress myself, or having someone clean me or feed me. The only people Dad knows are me and Mom.

I would never change the choice I made to take care of Dad. If only I could make him understand everything will be ok. I think things would be easier for all of us involved if he was just able to relax. The nonstop anxiety that he suffers with is the hardest thing to see him go through. He is continuously opening and shutting the front door, literally every five to ten minutes all day, and even into the night because he thinks someone is outside trying to come in and get us. At times we go multiple nights with no sleep because he is having these episodes of paranoia.

Dad literally doesn't even know where his bedroom or bathroom is. I help him put food to his mouth, help him go to the bathroom and brush his teeth. Not too long ago, he was able to wash his own hair. Now he can no longer even do that. He is literally nonstop. I need to focus on so many things to get done, but I feel so overwhelmed at times. I try to remember everything I need to do, but my mind is consumed with making sure Dad feels safe.

05 September

Something amazing happened today. Mom, Dad and I were sitting in the living room listening to music. Mom was doing her crossword puzzle when I noticed Dad waving at something. He was sitting in his chair looking over at the fireplace, waving. I looked over, but saw nothing. He had this real peaceful smile on his face. I asked him who he was waving at and he replied, "The man up there." I asked; "What man?", and he just continued to wave and smile over by the fireplace. He got real serious and spoke to whoever he was seeing. He said, "I am not scared. I am not running away, it's just that I am not ready yet." Mom and I looked at each other with our mouths open, shocked at what we just heard. I asked Dad again who he was speaking to. I saw nothing but peace and amazement on his face at whatever he was seeing. His eyes looked like he was somewhere else and he replied, "The man above."

By the peaceful look on Dad's face, we knew that what he was seeing was for real. We felt it, we saw it, and we heard Dad's words. Watching him wave and smile so happily at what he was seeing, we knew that he was having a conversation with the Man above.

06 September

Mom, Dad and I went to Knott's Berry Farm to have their chicken dinner for lunch. We were waiting in line when Mom brought to my attention Dad having these twitches or jerks to his left side. So I watched and I know that the doctor said as time goes on, Dad will have new onset of symptoms. To keep Mom calm, I told her what the doctor said, and we decided that it would be best to take Dad home just in case anything worse happens, especially since we did not know what to expect next or if his symptoms were going to get worse.

Later in the evening I went in to give him a kiss goodnight and I saw him facing his bed, bent over, arms straight, pushing with both hands down on the bed. As I came to Dad's side, I touched his arm and he was soaking wet. I asked him if he was ok but he didn't answer. He just continued with pushing down on the bed. I noticed his mouth and lips pulled in tight, his face was dark red and he was breathing deeply through his nose. I asked him once again if he was ok. He mumbled something but, I could not understand. I asked him to sit down. He was very off balance, especially to his left side. I sat him in his chair next to his bed and looked at him. He did not look good at all. I got Mom and let her know what was happening and asked what we should do.

Many times in the past, Mom, Dad and I spoke about CPR and hospital care but now that it was really happening, I needed to know once again what we should do. Even though it was a hard decision, Mom and I agreed to Dad's wishes that no matter what he doesn't want to go to any hospital and that he wants to die at home.

All of a sudden, his head fell back and he took one last deep breath in and stopped breathing. His face turned purple, his lips dark blue; his eyes rolled back in his head. I looked at Mom and Mom stared back at me in disbelief. I screamed. I felt his artery in his neck and there was nothing. I yelled Dad again, but no response. I screamed "Mom, Dad's not breathing!" All I could hear was Mom saying over and over, "Oh my God, oh my God George." I continued to scream, "Dad, Dad, please Dad, please breathe!" I said to Mom, "Dad's dead, he's not breathing!" His eyes were wide open and fixed with no life in them. His legs were purple all the way up to the knees, and his fingers were white with the nail beds almost black. Mom sat on the bed, tears flowing down her face and I stood by Dad, both of us shocked by what just happened. Minutes passed and I knew I had to make phone calls. As Mom and I sat there looking at Dad. I noticed his color changing. The purple color was now becoming pink along with his lips becoming lighter. I looked at his hands and the nail beds were no longer black but a healthy pink. He then took a deep harsh breath in and his head came forward. He looked dazed. I asked him if he was ok. Did he have pain anywhere? He told me in a weak slurred voice that he had pain in his head. I asked him if he wanted to go to the hospital. He told me and Mom no hospital.

I can't believe what just happened. Dad stopped breathing for a good 2 to 3 minutes and now he is back breathing again.

All we could do for Dad was put him in bed and say to ourselves "what now?" I still cannot believe that he took his last breath and came back; how mentally draining. That night I slept at the end of his bed, too scared to leave him alone.

07 September

Dad had what looked like another small stroke today. He is restless and I feel so bad for what is happening to him. I tried to take him outside in the sun, but he was just too unsteady on his feet, so I sat him on the back porch and Mom and I put on some music. Music always lifts his spirits, especially when we play Johnny Cash.

08 September

It's a little after midnight and I can still feel Dad shaking me. Finally after an hour of trying to get outside, he is back in bed. I had to put the couches in front of the door so he couldn't get outside. For the first time, Dad has gotten violent with me. I am so scared, not of him, but what is to come. Mom and I are so tired. We can't keep staying up like this. I can't believe it is has gotten to this level. I cannot believe his strength. My arms are still throbbing and burning and I cannot stop crying. His eyes scared me the most; they were glazed over, like he was possessed. Before he would just get agitated, but now it has turned physical. I don't want to lose my Dad. I laid back down on the couch hoping and praying Dad sleeps long enough for me to get some sleep myself.

After all this time watching Dad suffering, I realized I was being selfish to want him to live forever. I was only thinking of me, not him. Every night I would pray and ask God and Dad himself to stay strong and don't give up. But I never realized that with the battle he is fighting his suffering will never end till he takes his last breath.

Dad scared us bad today. He stopped breathing again, not just once but twice. Seeing him stop breathing, his face turn purple, his eyes roll back in his head, and his fingers turn almost black over and over again is just too much. Mentally it is breaking us. I feel so bad for him having to go through this.

Later in the evening he developed whole body jerks, especially in his head area. And he is still not eating or drinking. Sometimes these jerks are so strong I get scared that they will injure him. He keeps asking me to take him home. He is very restless and when I explain that he is home it seems at times he doesn't even know I am there. He just looks around trying to find where he thinks he should be.

09 September

This is the second night of Dad being physical with me. This time he left bruises on my arms. Luckily it did not last long. We let him be. Mom and I sat and watched making sure he didn't get hurt. The more we would try and stop him, the more aggressive he would become. I had to once again put the couches in front of the door. I prayed that he would just exhaust himself; thank God, our prayers were answered. This episode lasted only a little over an hour this time. He finally agreed to come back to bed.

After what looks like a small stroke, he can no longer swallow pills. I told Mom I have no problem feeding him. He is also now becoming more incontinent during the day; at least two times a day. I want to stay away from diapers for now because diapers cause the skin to break down and open up. He is having constant body jerks. He is complaining of head pain and is still not eating or drinking. His body is very hot with temperatures reaching almost 104 at times.

As Dad slept, Mom and I spoke in length about what the near future will hold for him and what we will do when he decides to stop eating. Mom spoke of putting a feeding tube in his nose to feed him. There is high probability of him pulling it out, and if that happens then we will have to put him in wrist restraints. We talked about if it is even ethical to do that. As each situation happens, we will be prepared to make decisions that will be best for Dad and his Alzheimer's. We will speak with hospice and a priest and honor his wishes of not prolonging his suffering.

For me personally, if I am suffering to the point of not knowing where I am, who I am, who others are that I have known for so many years, let me die when my body says I have had enough and it's ready to shut down.

Dad is 83 years old and he always told Mom and me that he has lived his life and when it is time to go, than it is time to go. He has also told Mom and I on many occasions that he does not want any extra measures taken like CPR if his heart should stop beating or if he should stop breathing, and he also doesn't want any feeding tubes. We will continue to love him, feed him, clean him, and keep him safe; whatever we need to do to keep him comfortable. When it is my time to leave this earth, this is exactly how I would want it to be.

10 September

Early morning I heard a loud sound like something heavy fall on the floor in Dad's room. I ran to his room and I found him under the stationary bike soaked in urine and incoherent. I washed him up. I can't stop crying. When I was putting clean clothes on him, he could hardly stand up, and his body and his recent jerks are even worse today.

I stood there watching his body jerk. He heard me crying and I will never forget the look he gave me. His jerks all of a sudden stopped and he looked up at me, smiled, put his hand out to me waving his hand slightly up and down like its ok, and he looked me in my eyes and smiled letting me know that he is going to be ok, and then went back to jerking . But everything is not ok. I can't do this. I can't handle watching him disappear little by little every day right in front of me. I need my Dad for just a little longer.

I put him back to bed since it was still early morning. I am laying here next to him listening to him breathe. Watching him suffer like this is by far the worst thing I have been through in my life. This is the third day that so far he has not eaten. I know that if things continue the way they are with him not eating, he will be dead in less than ten days.

Once again later in the day, he stopped breathing and has left-side full paralysis. I can't stand this. I can't stand to see him stop breathing only to keep coming back. It is torture for the three of us. Every time he takes his last breath, we say our goodbyes and then he comes back all over again and we get hopeful. This is too much for Mom and I. The extreme emotions that you go through when you watch your loved one stop breathing and then come back again over and over is a nightmare.

I can't help him. I can't save him. Mom and I can't do anything but watch. I love him so much; I don't want to let him go. This is my Dad who I am looking at, and I have to let him go each time he stops breathing. He is slowly dying and I can't help him. How much does God think we can take? I want to scream, "Dad wake up! Dad please wake up!" I want my Dad back so bad. I can't do this. My world is nothing without him.

I would gladly take all his suffering just to have him back the way he used to be. I will never hear him say "Yee haw" again after each joke, or put him in the front seat of my car to go on our daily errands. I will never see him at the dining room table to give him his meal or hear him say "Oh boy" when giving him his favorite dessert. I will never be able to take him to the beach, hold his hand and just listen to the waves. He will never come to my room again and kiss me good night and say "Tomorrow, same time, same thing?" or make me laugh in the store when he would let one rip and point at me saying I did it. Oh my God, please give me my dad back.

Since hospice has been brought in, they helped us put the bed in the living room to make taking care of Dad easier. Hospice has gathered all of the information for the mortuary so when it is time for Dad to leave this world, they will make that phone call that I know Mom and I would have a hard time making.

Hospice put Dad on medicine to keep him calm and sleep better at night, and brought in a nurse to help us bathe him a couple times a week. They are also there to listen to us and help us get through this last excruciating phase in his journey with Alzheimer's. Though they can't do what I need most - and that is save my dad - they are a Godsend. Without them, I know this would be a lot harder to deal with.

This is the second day that I am going to liquid fast. I believe in miracles. I need just one miracle, God, and I promise I will never ask for another.

11 September

Dad woke up fully responsive today with a clear mind (better than three years ago). It is so weird to hear him speak like nothing happened. What I love the most is how he still has some of his sense of humor. He has total left-sided paralysis, he is not able to eat, and is only requesting water. Hospice has started him on Seroquel and Morphine to make him calm and relaxed.

12 September

Dad's mind is still clear and he knows fully who we are. He is also requesting food and water, and this makes me so happy. He cannot walk or bend his left leg. I could not believe his appetite. Today he ate five eggs, two Greek yogurts, two applesauce, a turkey sandwich and mash potatoes, corn, peas and meatloaf. He is in such good spirits. Even through his suffering, he still stays positive.

13 September

Dad is joking all day today and he was able to tell us he loves us, and when he said "Yee haw" I cried. I thought I would never hear this again. He can now feed himself and he can even walk on his own. This is amazing. God blessed us with a miracle. It is just so weird that one day he stops breathing and the next he is walking on his own.

14 September

I woke up today and Dad is starting to regress back; OCD, insomnia, confusion, at times slurred speech and at times agitated. Mom and I make sure there are no loud noises and that it is light enough in the house so he doesn't get depressed, but dark enough to keep him calm.

15 September

Today Dad is joking a lot. But I notice after he wakes up he is at times clear of mind, happy, and calm for about 2 hours. I notice after that the agitation, obsessive compulsiveness and insomnia comes on. Only when I sedate him will he sleep and then wake up refreshed and happy. It is 3:00 pm and Dad is now sleeping deep with no signs of waking up.

16 September

It is 7:30 p.m. now and Dad has been sleeping since 3:00 pm yesterday. To watch him die right in front of us, alone, is one of the scariest times we have ever experienced in Dads journey with Alzheimer's. His breathing became labored, then turned to gasping, blue lips, gray pale skin and then his once beautiful blue eyes turned dull and solid with no life behind them. This will be imprinted in our minds forever. I had nightmares of his eyes for a long time. Till this day his lifeless eyes still haunt me in my dreams.

I will never forget checking for a pulse. I will never forget at the moment of each demise, how scared I became, how lost I really was. Working as an EMT with 911, I have seen many ways a human can die, but nothing prepared me to witness Dad die right in front of me.

This is day ten. I feel and see Dad's suffering. I got angry with God. Dad literally died four times only to come back again. This is messing with not only my mind but Mom's as well. This is literally torture on all three of us. It all feels so unreal. Dad's wishes were to die at home; I never thought that I would ever be asking God to take him now. To see him in bed dying, and then coming back, and being sedated; is wrong in every way.

Mom looked at me tonight; she has held her emotions in. We are different this way. I show my feelings and Mom holds most of hers in. She said to me, "I listen to you cry every day, all day, and I really worry for you when the day comes for Dad to go home." I told Mom, "I worry too." I never knew how strong a bond Dad and I had until I made the decision to put aside my life and job to take care of him full time. I continue to still pray for a miracle; but if it is God's will for Dad to be the way he is now, I am begging God to take him now because I literally can't take this anymore. Mom can't take this anymore and I know for sure Dad doesn't want another day of suffering.

I feel like I am in a nightmare that is replaying over and over again and it will not end. I can't watch him lay there basically every day like he is dead but still breathing. Why God? Seriously, why? I am going to miss this beautiful man who gave me five plus wonderful years that I was not able to get as a child. I think this is why I don't want to let go yet.

17 September

I woke up this morning to Dad's empty bed. I panicked, looked around frantically for him, and found him leaning against the kitchen counter, kicking back like old times. He stood there with his elbow on the counter, his left leg crossed over his right, just smiling away. This was truly amazing because he had full left-sided paralysis for about 4 days and now I am looking at him standing and leaning against the counter like nothing happened. I cannot believe he is walking on his own and he dressed himself in his jeans and his striped dress shirt like he always did when he would wait for me to take him to the store.

I was looking at him in amazement and he was just smiling, and then he gave me his famous wink. I said, "Dad your standing, you're out of bed!" He said, "Of course, why wouldn't I be?" I walked over to him and gave him a big kiss on his forehead. I sat him down and asked if he was hungry. He told me he was a little hungry. I laughed because he ate five eggs, a cup of applesauce and a cup of Greek yogurt. I sat with him and just stared at him as if he had just come back from a very long trip. I just couldn't believe all the suffering he has been through, and here he was sitting at the table eating and talking like nothing happened. I asked, "Do you know who I am?" Without hesitation he said, "You're my daughter." I then asked, "What is my name?" and he said "Jorge" and then he winked and smiled. I laughed so hard. Here is a man who continuously suffers but still continues to stay positive even after literally dying four times.

I am so happy right now. I have been sprinkling holy dirt from the shrine of El Santuario de Chimayo from New Mexico every day on Dad since this all started. I truly believe in miracles. I truly believe in prayers and I will always hold onto hope. He is not where he needs to be yet, but it doesn't hurt to have hope and believe that anything is possible through God. I am going to continue to ask God for a complete healing for Dad.

18 September

Dad is doing extremely well. I am still amazed at how well he is progressing. He continues walking and eating on his own after having left-sided paralysis. We walked him for about an hour today, and yesterday for 30 minutes. He gets weak and exhausted real quick but is still fighting the fight.

Dad had extreme tilting to his left side. We have seen a remarkable improvement within just days and he is now walking straighter and doesn't have as much of a hump in his upper back as he did from just yesterday.

He is eating five to six meals a day and drinking four 24oz bottles a day of spring water. He is also getting two freshly squeezed 32 0z vegetable juices a day. I am massaging every muscle in his legs, arms, neck, back, hips and feet four times a day every day to keep circulation good.

The biggest thing we are all noticing is that his thinking and conversation is like it was in 2007. Not 100% all of the time but a lot of the time. Even the conventional doctor could not explain why he is better than he was before. He also said it is amazing how Dad is now, especially after the video he looked at of him when he was suffering with what looked like a stroke last week.

I believe that the holy dirt, prayers, his healthy body and the will to live, along with me and Mom's around-the-clock care we have given him has kept Dad going.

Hospice has him on Seroquel two times a day at 50mg. We have actually separated and tweaked the dosages to 25mg, two times a day. This way Dad is not a zombie and he is actually interacting with us and not just lying in bed and not living.

Last night I lit a candle, meditated and prayed real deep, and said a Novena. I believe that through God all things are possible. Mom and I appreciate every day that we are blessed with Dad.

19 September

Dad slept all the way through last night. So far so good. The Seroquel is working really well. This morning I went to his bed, his eyes were open and he got this big smile on his face and right away he said to me, "I am just so happy to see you every time."

I kissed him and thought to myself, out of all that he has been through recently; I never thought I would hear him say anything to me; especially "I love you or "Yee haw." Moments like this mean the most to Mom and me.

Today Dad was able to walk to the bathroom with me by his side. I washed him up, shaved and dressed him, and now Mom and I and nephew Chris - who flew down from Colorado to help us for two weeks - will be going out for the day.

This is something else that I thought would never happen again with Dad. He is actually sitting next to me in the car. To have him in the front seat of my car like old times was the best thing I have had happen to me since this all started. I told Mom and Chris, if he is going to die it's not going to be lying in bed. I held Dad's hand as I drove toward the beach. He squeezed my hand and I looked over at him and he winked at me. I am truly the happiest woman on earth.

20 September

The hospice nurse and the on-call doctor made a house visit today. Both were amazed at Dad's progress. Both stated that in the years they have been in the medical profession, they have never witnessed the healing and reverse of symptoms like Dad's. Shockingly they both agreed that he is truly a miracle. He no longer has left-sided paralysis; he now walks and eats on his own. He speaks in full sentences. He no longer suffers with any head or body jerks. They both said they just cannot believe the difference between their last visits and now; he is almost 100% back to his old self. He still has some speech issues and some stuttering and finds it hard at times to put his thoughts into words.

21 September

I have been blessed with more time with Dad. When he is asleep I sit and listen to him breathe. I look at his young, almost wrinkle free skin. It looks like he is in his 60's, but he is 83. I look at his legs with muscles that would make younger men envious. He has so much physical life left in him, but his mind is betraying him. Two days in a row he literally made us laugh because he ran the length of the house along with the acre property. It was so funny because Lil Chris was following him, making sure he wouldn't fall when all of a sudden Dad did a football move by swinging around in a circle and bypassing Chris and then running the length of the house. Mind you, all he had on was a diaper and a T-shirt. I am so glad I was able to get that moment on video.

Dad is so young of mind. Mornings are his best times. He gives us about three to four hours of laughs, then he becomes extremely obsessive compulsive and aggressive if you stop him. About 20 hours' worth of Dad's daily life is consumed with worry, anxiety and OCD. We have had to up dosages on both morphine and Seroquel twice now in one week and today most likely we will have to up it again. This is not a way to live. I think what hurts the most is that I wanted to fix Dad so he could be around forever, but I know this can never happen.

Just this morning he said to me, "Good morning to you my little Hunny Bunny," and yesterday he said, "I feel so good when I see you." Everything he says to me I hold onto, because I know one day soon I am not going to hear those words anymore.

At this time I can no longer leave home for more than 30 minutes, even to visit friends. Dad becomes paranoid and scared. All of this is so very sad. Such a strong body, but his mind is so weak. He is also hallucinating when we give him the Seroquel. That is the only downside that I see about this medicine, but we have to do what we have to do to keep him calm. This medicine also helps with the body jerks.

I have learned a lot from Dad since I have been walking his journey with him with Alzheimer's. I will stick to the end even though at times I feel I am going to break. He will die at home, like he deserves to. I tell him every day that he will never be alone. He responds, "Oh thank God for you, I would be lost without you or Mom." I tell him that I would be lost without him. I am going to speak with God tonight. I hope once again he will hear me.

22 September

Dad is still progressing. He was able to go down the stairs with me just holding his hand. He was also able to put his feet in his shoes along with going to the bathroom by himself, pull up his pants, wash his hands, feed himself, and open doors. He also did four miles on the stationary bike. He almost got the whole alphabet. This is how he said the alphabet,"A, B, C, D, E, F, G, H, I, J, K, Bastard!" I laughed so hard. I told him that is not how you say the alphabet. He told me maybe not, but that is how he says it.

He definitely has sundowner's syndrome. He gets very anxious and agitated when the sun goes down. But he slept last night from 9:00

till 6:00 in the morning and we lowered his dosage of Seroquel from 50mg to 25mg with no more morphine. He is doing fine with no withdrawal symptoms, but then he has only been on it for a week. We are going to stop hospice soon, since he is no longer hospice material, and take him to a vascular neurologist next week and find out what is causing his strokes. I am thinking maybe the brain atrophy caused by the Alzheimer's. I noticed his speaking skills have been more mumbling. Maybe it's the medicine, or the strokes, or even the atrophy. We will hopefully find answers next week.

23 September

As of today, Dad is continuously progressing really well. He can now walk completely on his own along with eat and drink by himself. He no longer needs assistance going down stairs, getting himself in the car, or putting on his own seat belt. Per the nurse who visited today, he is totally lucid. He no longer has slurred speech and is no longer hallucinating. He is actually observing more and watches TV. He rode the bike today for four miles again.

26 September

We decided to take Dad off hospice. This will be the only way to be able to get him to see a Dr. If someone is on hospice they cannot go to the Doctor or hospital and since Dad is doing really well, we decided to find out what is causing these head and body jerks. He has a doctor's appointment next week. He is going to get a full workup including labs, and the following week at a neurology center. Mom and I are feeling really hopeful.

28 September

I found Dad standing in his room at five this morning, drenched in sweat and incoherent. Words were mumbled with jerking to his body and head. I called 911 and the medics came and brought Dad to the ER. They said his heart rhythm was not normal. He has AFIB (atrial fibrillation).

When we got to the ER, Dad was joking with everyone like nothing happened. He looked at me, smiled big and said, "Aw, there she is!" He then looked straight ahead and yelled out, "Yee haw!" A few seconds later he became non-responsive.

He had a full work-up in the ER of blood and urine testing, along with a CT scan and lung x-ray. The ER doctor came in and said Dad had

had no strokes. His heart and lungs are strong and healthy; blood work came out perfect along with no infections. But his brain is severely shrinking, causing his periodic non-responsiveness. He comes back strong and then, like today, non-responsive again.

What is so sad is that Dad can go another ten years because he has such a healthy body. His organs, including heart and lungs, are healthy. Nothing is enlarged according to the doctor. It is the Alzheimer's that is killing him. It hurts so badly to know that if he did not have this disease we could have him for so much longer.

I am not going to give up. We got Dad home about two this afternoon and he is still at this time unresponsive. The most ironic thing - and a true blessing - was that he was non-responsive in the ER the whole time all the way till discharge. Then they told us that the insurance will not authorize to have an ambulance take him home. I looked at the nurse and said out loud, "How are we going to get him home? He is not waking up and he has been in a deep sleep this whole time being here." All of a sudden like an alarm going off, his eyes opened and he sat up for us. The nurse put him in the wheelchair and wheeled him out to our car. He was able to get in the car with assistance and stayed awake till we got home. We got home 15 minutes later. Dad walked up the stairs with my help and got into bed and became instantly non-responsive within seconds. He fell into a deep sleep where he would not even answer me verbally or by physically. It was like he woke up when we needed him to. God is an awesome God. He has shown me and Mom over and over again that he is going to be by our side through this whole journey of Dad's.

Tonight I slept next to Dad at the foot of his bed. I could not leave him alone. Sleep was hard to get, but I could not let him be by himself.

30 September

It is 6:00 in the morning. Dad is in and out of responsiveness. Late last night he ate really well; he had two cups of applesauce, a cup of yogurt and about 18 oz. of greens drink. I don't understand how one day he is eating and walking, and the next he is in bed non-responsive.

It is 9:00 in the morning. I have never seen Dad so depressed. When he came to this morning, he said, "I just can't take this anymore!" and "I am so scared." This hurts to the core for Mom and me to hear these words coming from him.

I prayed to God to please give me his depression and any pain he is having. His body is jerking like someone who is having seizures.

I hate to see him suffer. I make sure that I do not feed his depression. I keep him in well-lit rooms or outside in the sun with low music and make sure to just be there when he needs me.

Right now he wants to be alone, and I understand where he is coming from because I know too well what that deep dark depression can do. I keep telling him he is not alone and we are with him. I told him I would be with him every step of the way. I laid on his bed next to him and I told him he is my best friend and that I love him more than anything, and that if I could I would take all of his suffering away.

It is late morning and Dad is not doing well. The body jerks are bad and I have to put him back on hospice. Finally after giving him some Seroquel, he is sleeping peacefully.

He got so much better and Mom and I thought he was good to go, and that he was back where he was before all these symptoms started. But we've come to realize that there is no getting better for him. He is angry and rightfully so. He is so frustrated, and for the first time I actually saw in his eyes no recognition for Mom or I or his house that he has lived in for almost 40 years. He told me that I am not his daughter and he didn't even know Mom. Even though I know it is the Alzheimer's, it still hurts so badly.

It is 3:00 in the afternoon and the hospice nurse just left. She couldn't stop complimenting on how healthy and young he looks. So he is back on hospice and there will be no more hospital visits or doctors' visits.

It is 8:00 at night and Dad just got done eating a Greek yogurt, 18 oz. of juice and two cups of applesauce. I love seeing him eat. I know deep down inside that this is just for now, but it still gives me some small hope that he will at least be around for the holidays.

He has not had a bowel movement for three days now. I did not want it to get to this point because at one time in the beginning when he started going downhill, I told Mom that no matter what I do not want to see Dad naked and that she will have to clean him when it gets to that point. Dad is a handful. Mom and I clean him, something that took some time to get used to for me. Now he is in another stage of this disease where he cannot move his bowels. So I had to assist him in having one, and even though I felt uncomfortable, I had to do it because I didn't want Dad to suffer with anything else that I can prevent from happening. This will not be a first time situation. As time goes on, and Dad becomes bed confined, the more I will have to assist him every two to three days to prevent a blockage in his intestines. When someone is on hospice, they are not allowed any hospital care or doctors' visits, so making sure he doesn't suffer in any way is a top priority.

01 October

Dad said two things to me today that he has never said to me any time in my 42 years on this earth. I asked him, "Who am I to you?" He said, "You are my everything." I told him that I love him and he said, "I love you more...I love you more than anything in this whole world....You are my everything."

I am so angry! So angry! My dad, my best friend, is suffering like this. He has had a 103 fever on and off for two days now. He sleeps about 20 hours a day. Mom and I cherish the four hours we have with him. What a rollercoaster of emotions to deal with.

October 02

I had to start using a vest restraint. I cannot let him hurt himself. Dad got out of his hospice bed two times last night when I dozed off. I heard movement and I shot up from the couch just in time to catch him before he fell all the way to the floor both times. His body is so hot and his eyes are so red from the high fever. Since last night he's been having these breathing episodes where he is gasping for air. I hate the sound; it saddens me that I cannot help him.

I have to let this nightmare, this endless torture, take its course. I feel so helpless and hopeless. The selfish part of me wants him to stay forever, but only if he would no longer suffer. I already feel empty inside and he is not even gone yet. I can't stop crying. I need him. Maybe, just maybe, if he was the dad I needed when I was growing up, it would be easier to let him go. I cherish every kiss and I can't hear him tell me he loves me enough because I want to hear those words forever. I just want to wake up from this nightmare and have Dad be all better.

04 October

Dad's fever finally broke. He still has a low grade fever of 100.3.

Mom and I gave Dad a bed bath. He is no longer walking on his own. As we give him a bed bath, Mom and I notice he is losing so much weight. His bones are becoming so pronounced. I hate this. You know he is unbelievable, he is a fighter and even though he is suffering he always seems to come through to lift our spirits. I get so excited when I see him in the morning. I say "Hi Dad!" and he grabs my hand, smiles, and over emphasizes "Goood morrrning!" I can tell he is so tired, especially when I look in his eyes. I can see that he is so ready for this battle to come to an end. But for whatever reason he is still here. Mom and I put on oldies, not too loud because Dad is very sensitive to loud noise.

Mom sat me down to speak with me. She is concerned about how Dad's passing will be. Will we be able to handle it? Will he suffer even more? She hasn't really spoken about it till now. Fear and reality is probably setting in. Mom and Dad have been together over 50 years. She doesn't know what she is going to do when it is all said and done.

I set up funeral arrangements yesterday because I know I will not be able to do anything when Dad passes. We found out that the funeral and the cremation were never paid for. This was a huge downer, because mom thought everything was taken care of. It shocked me because I am making funeral arrangements for him and he is still alive. I feel like I am betraying him because I am already planning something before it's even happened. I feel guilty; like I am already condemning him to death, but then I stop and realize that this is the best decision because it will be so much harder after his passing.

He is bed confined and barely able to walk with assistance to go to the bathroom. I carry him more than anything. I have assisted him to the bathroom for over a month on and off now. I put his right arm all the way over my shoulder and hold his hand for support with my left arm under his right arm around to the left side of his chest and we walk together to the bathroom. Every time we make this walk, Dad says the same things: "You know you are really a good person" and "If it wasn't for you, I would be lost" and "You really are my best friend." Each time I carry Dad to the bathroom I have to hide the tears to make sure he doesn't hear me cry. I never in a million years thought I would be carrying my dad to the bathroom and holding him up in front of the toilet so he could go to the bathroom like a man.

He was joking a few times yesterday. It felt so good to see him do this. The hospice nurse said that he has to be having small strokes because it only affects one side of his body. I told her that the ER doctors say there is no evidence on the CT results of any strokes. Who knows? One day Dad will have full use and the next it will be completely gone. I have been massaging Dad about four times a day still, and doing range of motion, so his joints don't get stiff. Dad loves these massages. Mom warms the lotion and she will get the top half of Dad and I take the lower half. He smiles the whole time when we are massaging him.

I put him to bed and I whispered in his ear that it is ok to go when he is ready and that Mom and I will be ok. His eyes snapped opened and he got this real angry face and said, "No, you said this before, I don't want to hear that anymore!" I said, "Ok Dad I will never say it again."

05 October

Dad always has the same symptoms before something bad happens. It starts with severe insomnia, panic, anxiety and loss of appetite. Last night, he was up all night. This morning he was eating some yogurt and told me he was sorry. I asked him what was he sorry for and he told me that he was a lot to take care of. I told him to never apologize and that I do not mind taking care of him. All of a sudden Dad said that I had to be careful because there is something going on in here. He pointed to the right front and side areas of his head. He said that there is a dark hole and it's empty in there. I told him that I will be careful. I need to remember to ask for the results of those scans from the hospital, in case maybe there is something to what he is telling me.

About 15 minutes ago he woke up and had full body tremors and jerks so bad it looked like he was having seizures again. I held him and told him I am not leaving him, that I would stay right here with him. I held his head in my arms and massaged his chest lightly. I am so saddened by his suffering. I don't want him to suffer anymore. Whatever route God should decide I don't want him to suffer another day.

It is so weird; Dad fell again yesterday. He walked normal all day yesterday and then today it's just the opposite. I wish he would sleep peacefully till he goes home with God, but right now it looks like the opposite. I am going to continue to pray for peace for him.

06 October

This is day 29 since Dad's decline in his mental and physical status. He is losing weight at a dramatic rate. He continues to have up and down days along with periodic high fevers. Just yesterday he had left-sided paralysis and today he is able to walk. His body and head have been jerking all day, and his appetite is light. He has episodes of depression, anger, sadness, and then happiness and still has a will to continue the fight. The one thing I cannot stand to watch is how his brain is slowly killing him. He told me yesterday that he is going to get better so he can start going with me again to run errands. This made me cry because I wanted to believe it so badly. I would love for him to be able to go in the car with me or go see a movie like we used to. But reality sets in and I know those days are gone forever.

Even though I hold onto hope and believe in faith and the power of God, my intuition tells me that he will never live and function normally in life again.

11 October

God answered one of our prayers today. Once again he was able to walk down the stairs and get into the car. It was so awesome to be at the lake with Dad and Mom again. This was definitely another miracle for the three of us. We are going to try for the beach on Friday...God willing. All of this is just so unbelievable and at the same time amazing and mentally draining.

Last night Dad looked at me, kissed my forehead, and told me he is so tired. I knew what he meant. I told him that I cannot do what he wants me to do. I could never just end someone's life; that is not a decision I could ethically make. I told him that I wish I could make him feel better, and he told me he knows I would. I told him that God would not give him anything he couldn't handle. He told me he knew this. I asked him if he speaks to God, and he told me he speaks with him every day. That right there made me feel so good. He does not need any medicine during the day, just a low dose at night.

Today I was able to get Dad in the shower for the first time in a month. His mood changed, he became lucid and started joking around. So I got him dressed and brought him out to the living room. Mom had oldies on. Johnny Cash was playing "A boy named Sue" and all of a sudden, Dad grabbed me, held my hands...And just for a moment, for the first time in my life, we danced. He held me and then twirled me and then stopped. I needed this. I needed to dance with my father just once in my life before he goes home forever. I am the happiest girl in the world.

15 October

Dad was 165 pounds on September 13th. It is October 15th and he is now 139 pounds. His skin is hanging from his arms and legs. He basically has no muscle left. I can see his ribs and back bones through his shirts and his knees are basically just skin. He sleeps most of the day. This is literally the most depressing thing Mom and I have ever gone through; except for watching him die in front of us repeatedly.

We are literally watching Dad physically deteriorate in front of us.

He is dying a slow death. Mom and I are staying strong and we make sure we do not cry in front of him. A few times I could not hold back and he would grab my face and kiss my forehead and say "Shhhhh." I hug him and kiss him every chance I can get, and tell him he is not alone and that Mom and I will be with him forever. I have not slept in my bed for over a month now. I sleep on the couch next to Dad's hospital bed and make sure he knows he is not alone.

He can no longer walk on his own. He has no energy from all the muscle loss. He can walk with me if I hold him up. I half carried him to the car because today Mom, Dad and I made it to the beach. Even though Dad could only leave the car for a minute, it was priceless to see the smile on his face when he realized that he was at his favorite place. I was able to carry Dad outside the car and lean him up against the car. Mom stood on the other side and held him up while I took a picture of them facing the ocean. Just that little bit of exertion was all Dad could take. I had to put him back in the car and went back home. He was exhausted and I was a little nervous because I did not want anything bad to happen in the car.

Today, Dad told me he was only going to heaven if I was going. Our bond is so deep. I would spend my whole life dedicated to him if I knew he was not going to suffer the way he is now. I would literally put my life aside forever for Dad and Mom.

18 October

Mom came to me. She was scared. This is the first time I have seen her like this. She told me she did not want him to go out this way by starving to death. She asked if we could get him a high calorie protein drink.

He is now on 3000 to 4000 calories a day. He has gone from 139 to 141 in three days. I will weigh him again in three more days. The past few days have been good ones for him, but today was not good. He is extremely lethargic. I think it's because we let him get up a lot, using a lot of energy.

My back is hurting from carrying him to the bathroom numerous times a day, every day. Some say to just put him in a diaper to make it easier on me, but I can't. If he wants to go to the bathroom like a man instead of just lying in bed all day in a diaper, then I will do it. I want him to continue to feel like the strong man he was his whole life for as long as possible.

He slept the second half of the day away. We get him outside in the sun every day for an hour or so. It is so sad to see him never at peace. He has gotten to the point where he cannot relax long enough to stay in the house. When he wants to go outside because his anxiety is so high from being in the house, Mom and I will bring him outside hoping it will bring him some peace, but it only lasts about 15 minutes. Then his anxiety kicks in and he wants to come back inside. No matter what, his mind will not let him relax either way.

I tried to get back to the point of living my life again and getting excited about celebrating my birthday, but I just can't do it. I get out about two days a week for about an hour total but I feel guilty every time I leave because of Dad gets so anxious. When I leave he says, "Please come back home safe, I need you."

I know life ends in death. It doesn't matter. I am trying very hard to accept what will come, but I can't see my life without Dad, I can't. I am tired of leaving without Dad with me. I am tired of people asking where Dad is when I go to the stores we used to frequent. I have a hard time passing the bakery where Dad would pick his favorite chocolate donut or glazed twist, or going to the park or lake where we would walk every day.

I am so tired. I am so scared, sad, and empty without Dad. I want him here for a while longer. Just give me another year. Just give me one year where he doesn't suffer with panic and anxiety. Just one year of happiness, true happiness, where he knows nothing but peace. To live and be happy with no worries, no fear.

For the first time I see fear in Moms eyes. She made me so proud the other night when she gave Dad a kiss, a real kiss. I had never seen that in my whole life. Then Dad asked her for two more. I love Mom for being my rock. I love her for being there for me when I went through my seven month nightmare in 2009. To this day she still tries to comfort me and help me where she can with Dad. I promised her that she will never be alone and I will make her wishes come true when it is time.

24 October

Dad was not doing well yesterday or today. I noticed a change in him yesterday. He does not want to eat. He woke up this morning and is not in a good place. He wants to kill himself. He said, "I wish I could just jump off a cliff!" I just held him and told him I am so sorry and I wish I could take his suffering away. He is so angry, he told us to leave him alone. I know he doesn't mean it, but he is just so frustrated and I do not blame him. So I put him back to bed, made him comfortable, and just let him be.

I feel guilty; guilty for begging him to eat even when he doesn't want to. I feel guilty that just maybe I am prolonging his suffering. I feel selfish to want him to stay around longer because I can't handle the fact that life without him would be so empty. I know he is suffering. I know that no one deserves to suffer like this, and that the right thing to do would be to just let him be. It is so hard to let go of a man that I have grown to love more than myself. Mom says that I don't even take care of myself anymore. I just want to make him better, make him happy again. I just want him to be able to walk outside with me and go wherever, like we used to do. I just want everything to be back to the way it was. I can't stop crying. I don't want him to suffer anymore either way.

Hospice was here today. The nurse told me that she can see a huge decline in Dad. Due to the massive muscle loss, not eating or drinking, etc., she doesn't expect him to last another week. He has shocked us all in the past, so who knows when it will be time. Seeing his body when I change his diaper just makes me feel hopeless. He looks like he just came out of a concentration camp. This man, who has only a 10th grade education, who taught himself to became a Chief Engineer on an oil tanker for the largest oil company in the world, held many titles and medals in Olympic Powerlifting, is now basically confined to bed. Now, this disease, this curse, is slowly killing him in less than two months. He could run in the park just two months ago, and now he is basically bed confined. All of this is just so overwhelming.

26 October

Yesterday was a really good day for Dad. He walked, yes walked, at least 10 times in the house, consumed about 3000 calories, enjoyed an hour out in the sun, and laughed and joked with us.

Today he has slept all day. Even with little exertion he got extremely winded. He looked pale and his fingers turned almost black and then went back to the healthy pink. I truly think his heart is going. He has refused all water and food and continues to be in a deep sleep. Deep down inside I feel his time is near, but I still keep hoping for a miracle. I don't want to give up on the power of God, but I also get the feeling that what God wants for Dad is something different from our wants. Regardless, even though it is going to be so traumatic for Mom and me, we do not want him to suffer anymore.

I hugged him today and all I felt was his ribcage. I hate this. I prayed to God that if he will not give a total healing, then please take him before he becomes a skeleton. This is one thing Mom and I cannot stand to see. I feel useless because there is nothing more I can do for him. I love him enough to let him go, even though I do not want to. I have a feeling that he will not be with us for the holidays. This is so hard to accept. I wish this was a nightmare so I could wake up and Dad would be ok. I love you Dad, so much, I just wish I could keep you forever.

30 October

Dad has had four good days straight. Last Wednesday, the hospice nurse felt that he was not going to make another week. Today when I came back from the store, he was waiting by the door to greet me. I never thought I would see this again. I was even happier when he gave me his big smile and waved and said, "There's my girl, there she is!"

God has blessed me so much. Some people have told me that this is basically just a fluke, and that it will not last. Others in the medical field have said that they have seen this behavior to a certain extent, but never has someone had good and bad days this long. I say no one knows what God has in store for him. I will take every day and every blessing that God gives us, and accept the good and the bad that will come with the reality of Dad's demise.

He is walking on his own again today, but still needs assistance sitting on the toilet and going up and down stairs. If he should continue to have good days, I am going to start him on lifting low weight dumbbells for his upper body and do the bike for his lower body. He still has some left-sided weakness. He cannot touch his face with his left hand, but he can grasp objects with some difficulty. He has no problems swallowing. He is actually more lucid then he was three years ago. This in itself is amazing. The only thing we need to work on now is Dad getting up through the night. Mom and I are losing a lot of sleep. I am only getting about two straight hours at a time every night. If I wasn't juicing and eating right, I know I would never be able to continue with the care of Dad.

Today once again Dad was smiling with a peaceful smile, waving toward the fireplace. I heard him say out loud, "I'm coming home soon." For some reason I was somewhat shocked to hear what he had just said. I asked him what he was waving at and who he was talking to. He looked at me. He looked so happy and he said, "My Mom. I told her I am coming home soon." Tears filled up in my eyes because I knew that what he was saying was true.

31 October

Dad woke up early this morning in pain after almost 18 straight hours of deep sleep. His tremors and body jerks are back, but this time they are extremely severe. They literally look like a mixture of seizures and turrets syndrome. Every time he comes back after one of these episodes, he is never where he needs to be. He will have nonstop anxiety, panic, and worry.

He said to me today, "Please help me, please help me get home, please do something, help me please, I don't know what to do or how, please help me!" I knew what he meant and what he wanted me to do once again. He had tears streaming down his face, begging me, looking me straight in the eyes and pleading with me to end his life for the third time. I want to scream. I want to run away and not face what's to come. Dad can't take anymore, I know this, and I can't and won't do what he wants me to do. I gently tell him to please don't ask me to do that anymore. He tells me he is sorry and that he will not ask anymore. I held him and told him I will make sure he sleeps. God, this is killing me to see my Dad look me in the eyes and beg me to end his suffering. I have never felt so defeated in my life. For the first time I did not know what to do or say except to hold him. I wanted to end his suffering somehow, but definitely not take his life. I wonder, if I was in his situation would I ask someone to do the same thing for me? I really don't know. I will say this much: I would never want to suffer as long as he has. Even though I know he is suffering, I could never make the decision to end his life. So I comfort him with love and morphine and pray to God for a miracle or to take Dad home now and take his suffering away. Dad, if I could, I would do whatever I could to take your suffering away. I hope you forgive me. The worst kind of suffering is to watch someone else suffer and knowing you can't do anything about it.

Today is the day that I finally told myself no more. Let him be and stop being selfish. I will no longer beg him to eat or drink. I will no longer ask him to do anything. Somehow even though I know it's in God's hands, Dad held on for Mom and me because I selfishly cried and begged him to stay. He even told us that he was scared to go because he was worried about Mom and I being alone. I was in denial this whole time, thinking he could be cured. Mom accepted and was ready from the beginning, because she was never in denial like I was. Even now I sit back and picture living life without Dad and it instantly brings hard core tears. Just sitting here thinking about it, I feel so guilty for expecting him to live this way when in fact I would never want this for myself for a second.

This afternoon, his heart and breathing stopped, and then came back once again. His fingers were blue and his breathing was labored, and then stopped all together. He cries out in pain. I am scared for him. I don't want him to go, but that is the only way to end his suffering.

Before Dad went into a deep sleep, he looked into my eyes and told me I can go to heaven with him. To be honest, I wouldn't mind at all. I asked Dad, with God's permission, to please come back and visit me when he gets to heaven, just so I know he is ok. I will feel better knowing he is safe and that he made it home. He promised he would come and visit me.

Mom and I have continued taking care of Dad's business. This will make things a little easier when the time comes for him to go home.

01 November

I can't sleep. I lay here listening to Dad breathe and the clock tick away on the wall. Day three of no food. I prayed that it wouldn't get to the point of being able to see every detail, every outline, of Dad's bones pressing against his skin. Mom and I feel for him and wish that we could take his suffering, at least some of it, away. Mom cried hard yesterday for the first time. Everything is coming to the surface now for her. I feel for her too. 50 plus years together and sometime next week, Dad will be gone. To even think that you can know when your loved one is going to die is one of the most depressing, crazy things one can go through. Sometime next week, Dad will be gone forever. In a way, it is still unreal to me. I still think there is a possibility that he will wake up and everything will be ok again.

02 November

In the morning I stood by Dad's bed. He looked up at me and said, "Well hello there, Baby." Then he got real serious, looked into my eyes and said, "You are every reason why I am still here. I love you." He turned his head and fell into a deep sleep once again. His words touched me deeply.

This afternoon he came to and found Mom standing over him, crying. He looked up, reached for Mom's hand, and kissed it and told her he loves her. What a beautiful moment. Mom said she needed that. She asked me if I saw the peaceful glow on his face, and I told her yes.

I became frantic today. The should have's, the maybe's, the could have's. So I called Mom's cardiologist. This man is a beautiful soul. I asked him to save my Dad, because I know he has some kind of heart blockage. And I asked if he could just open his artery and save him like he saved Mom. I told the doctor that he will get better after surgery because the blockage is probably causing his forgetfulness, confusion, etc. The cardiologist did not laugh at me or ridicule me. He told me to bring Dad in. I was shocked. I was expecting the total opposite. This gave me so much hope. I then told the doctor of Dad's symptoms and that he is now bed confined, going into full arrest multiple times, lucid one moment and totally incoherent other times. The doctor told me that he believes even if someone has Alzheimer's, they should still be treated like a human being, but when someone is suffering to the extent Dad is, I need to let go. The phone became silent as I really listened to his words and they sunk in. I knew then that I was at a point where I know Dad is close to going and I was still trying one last time to save him. One last chance maybe to stop what was to come. As I hung up the phone I felt so defeated.

03 November

This morning Dad is not in a good place. He looked at me and told me he doesn't know what to do. I told Dad that right now Mom and I are taking care of everything and there is nothing to worry about. He continued to say "I am tired, I am so tired." I told him that I will put him back in bed and he can go to sleep. He said "No, I mean I am tired" and kept looking at me. I said, "Dad I can't do what you want me to do, but I can make you sleep till you go home." I asked him if he would like that, and with no hesitation he said, "Yes please, I want to sleep!"

Today Mom, Dad and I came to an agreement that we will sedate Dad till he goes home. But when he comes to, we will offer food and water, and if he doesn't want anything we will then sedate him again to keep him comfortable.

Tonight I went to his bed and bent over to kiss him goodnight. I grabbed his hand and kissed his right cheek, and that is when I noticed a slight cool, peaceful wind. Not enough to blow my hair, but a circling breeze around us. I looked around for the source. All of the windows were closed and there were no fans on. I asked Mom if she had the air on and she told me no. I felt a light energy around us. It was almost like we were in a different place, a different dimension. It felt very light and very peaceful. When I let go of Dad's hand to walk away the cool breeze, the energy, was gone.

04 November

More than anything in the world, I would love for us to go to the movies just one more time.

This morning I approached Dad's bed and once again I can feel a different energy around him; almost like he is not here anymore, but still breathing. He has a grayish look to him, his mouth won't close; this part I have grown to dislike. His eyes are no longer the beautiful blue eyes he once had, but a dull cloudy look. When I saw this, I got very angry and asked God to take him already. Almost two months now. I know there is no getting better. I accept this now. I can't believe that Mom and I have not gone crazy through all of this. It's almost time for him to go home. I feel it coming, I see it coming. I feel really empty inside, but on the other hand Dad will no longer suffer. His suffering needs to come to an end. This is just too much for Mom and me. He is no longer talking or walking and if he does talk, it is just whispers. He can no longer swallow. Out of everything, I wish to hear his precious voice again.

All I do is cry. I could be shopping for food or Dad's supplies and all of a sudden a memory of him will make me cry right there. I try and hold it in till I get outside, but sometimes it is just so hard. I miss Dad in my car. This is the hardest, especially when I close the gates and I can see him lying in bed not going with me, wondering if he thinks I left him behind. Sometimes I want to just come back, walk in the house, pick him up and take him with me and hope and pray that he will wake up and sing to the music that I have always played for him. Coming back is even harder, because inside I never want to give up. And even now in the shape Dad is in, I expect to walk in the door and find him sitting in the chair, laughing with Mom. And he would say, "Hey there's my girl," get up and walk toward me, and ask to go for a ride.

This is all just so depressing, and even though I am very spiritual and I know there is a better place, I still have to stay behind because I know I will be here to take care of Mom. She needs me now. I know this and this is what keeps me going. She looks so tired but she is such a strong woman.

I left today to fill out the rest of the cremation papers, but once again I wasn't able to finish because the head guy wasn't there and I really didn't feel comfortable continuing with the legal documents till the owner comes back. Just getting there exhausted me. To walk into a mortuary was very eerie and draining. You can feel way too much at one time, very overwhelming. I have faxed over what I need to for Mom's medical benefits when Dad should pass, and now a few more papers to be filled out and I will be done. I'm going to try and complete it at Kinko's tonight and bring it back tomorrow

05 November

I went over to Tamra's house tonight and I was able to complete all the paperwork for Dad's cremation. The only thing left was Mom's signatures at the mortuary. This is a big stress relief, especially since I know that when it is all said and done and Dad has been taken home, Mom and I will not be able to handle anything for a while.

On the way home from Tamra's house I just cried. I screamed over and over again. I felt so much pain. I thought to myself, my Dad is going to be leaving soon. This man that Mom and I took care of for five years and five months will be physically leaving us. It was basically just the three of us, every day for so many years. Not a day went by that Dad did not make us laugh, and even when it was so hard at times to take care of him, he loved us. He loved us unconditionally. I got home and right away I went to Dad's bed. I kissed his forehead. I was expecting him to be dead for some reason, but was so happy when I heard him breathing. Even though he was not responsive, I let him know that I will sleep right here next him and that I love him.

06 November

Early morning, Dad is still here with us and I was finally able to try and give him some medicine to make him sleep because of his endless loud sighing all night. He sounded so uncomfortable. I mashed the pills up and he was able to swallow. I massaged his whole body after changing his diaper. I could tell he felt so good and relaxed while doing this. When I was massaging his legs, I noticed that my hands were leaving imprints in his skin like memory foam, all the way up to his groin area. And his skin color is now a light yellow. I think his kidneys are failing. I just kept massaging him and I looked to see if he fell back to sleep, but he was looking at me. Even though his eyes were dull, I can tell he knew it was me. I said, "Does this feel good Dad?" Dad couldn't close his mouth all of the way so he lightly whispered, "Yesss." He looked me in my eyes, weakly smiled, and then winked. I said "I love you so much Dad." Dad weakly whispered, "I love you more."

No More Suffering

07 November 2012

This morning I approached Dad's bed and I could feel a different energy around him, almost like he is not here anymore, but still breathing. He has a greyish, pale look to him.

I shaved Dad today because I knew from last night's visitation that today was his day to go home. He always prided himself on how he looked, how he dressed, and always having a clean shave.

As I was shaving him, I couldn't stop crying. He's lost so much weight; the skin on his face was literally the outline of the bones on his face. Because of this, I nicked his face four times and for some reason this made me cry even harder. The whole time I took care of him, I proudly made sure he didn't have pressure marks on his body from being in bed for long periods.

Not too long ago, he would look me in my eyes as I shaved him and periodically wink at me. Shaving him right now was bringing back so many bittersweet memories. I would shave him every two days. What I missed the most is when Dad would make faces or wink as I shaved him. In between laughing, I would tell him to stop and he would say "Ok, ok" and he would be serious for only a minute, and then he would make those faces again. I just realized that this will be the last time I will ever shave his face.

He came to a little as I massaged his body after changing his diaper. Two months ago this man had so much muscle on his body, and now when I changed his diaper I could even see his pelvic bone. He literally looked like he just came out of a concentration camp. I could tell by his face that he felt so good and relaxed while I was massaging him. With a dull faraway look in his eyes, he looked at me and tried to say something, but only a whisper came out. I asked him to repeat what he said. Once again he tried, but I just couldn't understand him because his voice was now only a very light whisper. In between sobs, I begged him to please talk to me and tell me what he was trying to say because I couldn't understand. I just collapsed with desperation on his chest and cried. I needed so desperately to hear what he was trying to say to me. I looked up at him and he looked down at me with a frown on his face. I said, "Please, please I need to know what you said!" I repeated my words again as he looked down at me. His voice was gone. The thing I wanted the most was to hear Dad's voice, not a whisper, but his voice. I miss his voice so bad. Dad's voice is gone forever. He said "Shhhh, shhhh" as he caressed my hair and weakly rubbed my shoulder and back. Then he fell back to sleep.

I was sitting on the couch when I saw him lurch forward, and dark brown liquid came out of his mouth. I jumped up and turned him on his side to make sure he would not choke on his own vomit. Mom came over and we changed his shirt, cleaned his face, and sat next to him. I watched him breathing and noticed his breathing was now rapid. His respirations were now at 44 per minute, while normal breathing is 14 to 20 per minute. I felt for his heart rate and it was 160. He was drenched with sweat. Working on the ambulance, I knew that his time to go home was very close. It was about 12 in the afternoon when I decided to call hospice. I knew it was time. Kim from hospice showed up 30 minutes later to evaluate Dad. I didn't want her here. Not because I didn't like her, but because of what she was there for. I didn't want to face this. If I told her to leave maybe he wouldn't die. I knew this wasn't rational, but it was how I felt at the time.

His breathing started to dramatically slow down. Mom and I couldn't stop crying. His breathing was now at 4 breaths per minute. I got up and sat on the left side of Dad, Mom on the right. Mom held his hand. I got close to him and spoke to him. I said, "Dad I love you so much! Don't be scared, you're not alone. I love you Dad. I love you, I love, I love you! We're right here! Mom and I are right next to you! We're not going to leave you!" I tried not to cry, but it was so hard to see this man that I have grown to love more than even myself, leaving Mom and I. Mom said, "George I love you! I love you George! Thank you for loving me the way you do. Thank you for all the good memories." She couldn't say anymore. She held Dad's hand and kissed him. She cried hard. For the first time in 50 plus years, Mom was to losing her best friend.

As Dad's breathing became slower and more spaced apart, stopped and then started again, I looked at his eyes. I will never forget his eyes. They became fixed and solid, dull with no life left in them. I saw his throat going up and down. He was trying to get more breaths in, and then everything became quiet. Everything stopped. His chest stopped rising and falling. His throat stopped moving. He was gone. Dad was gone.

Dad took his last breath at 1:05 p.m.

No matter how many times we closed his eyes, they would open again and his mouth was stuck wide open like a silent scream. It was too much. I could not stand the sight of Dad's eyes and mouth permanently open. Mom couldn't handle another minute.

Mom and I cried so hard. We kissed his hands and his face. Even though he suffered the last two months of his life and we no longer wanted him to suffer anymore, we couldn't believe he was gone. Even though he was still in his bed, the house was so empty. Kim from hospice asked when we wanted him to be taken away. Mom and I said right away, because we couldn't handle his eyes and mouth not closing. It was just too much for us.

Kim asked me and Mom, since Dad was only wearing a diaper, if we wanted to dress him before the mortuary came for him. I washed down his body with holy water before we put him in his favorite blue jogging pants and one of his favorite weightlifting T shirts. When we were done, I asked Kim to help me get a lock of hair from him. We took off his wedding ring and the scapular of Our Lady of Guadalupe. Mom put his ring next to her ring on her finger, and I put on the Scapular.

We heard the van from the mortuary pull up. I asked Mom and Kim if I could be alone with Dad for a minute, and when they left I bent over and whispered in his ear,

"Don't forget your promise, Dad. With God's permission I will be waiting for you."

I kissed his forehead, his cheeks, his hands, and next to his mouth, and I whispered, "I love you Dad."

When they came to get him, Mom and I stayed out on the back porch. We couldn't handle the site of them putting him in a bag and taking him away. When I heard the gurney come in the house, the clicks of the gurney being lowered and the two men putting him on the gurney, I couldn't take it anymore. I gagged and dry heaved. I knew this was reality.

Everyone was gone. Mom and I looked around the living room. We couldn't believe Dad was gone. The house felt so empty; so quiet without his loud breathing. We cried and just looked around then at each other. It felt so weird. For so many years our daily lives were filled with the 24/7 care of dad, and now everything came to a standstill; just like that everything was quiet and still. When Dad took his last breath, I wished right then that I had taken mine too.

The Visits

To this day I expect Dad to come out of his room and say, "Just kidding, I'm back!" The house is so eerily quiet. I cannot accept what has happened with Dad. I stand in the middle of the living room where his bed used to be and feel alone and empty inside.

It was just the three of us every day for almost six years. Sitting on this couch where I slept next to Dad for the last two months of his life brings back so many bittersweet memories. Staring at the clock on the wall that was so loud the last 12 hours of Dad's life, now I can barely hear it tick away.

In a way I wish I could turn back the hands of time to a day where Dad could dress himself and walk down the stairs get in the car and go to the beach or the movies with me. But then I would have to relive those last hours watching him struggle to take his last breaths. Seeing his throat go up and down trying to take just one more breath before giving in would be just too much to go through again. After he passed, I once again journaled for the next month and a half because he continued to visit and comfort us both from the other side on a daily basis in some way.

07 November - Wednesday

I heard your voice tonight, Dad. Mom and I heard little noises and we heard your voice call out to us. You sounded so far away, but I knew you were there. Your voice was not the Alzheimer's voice, but before when you were so strong and healthy. The energy in the house is so heavy. Your spiritual presence is so heavy in the house, Dad. Even though you are gone physically, we can feel you here like you were here before you took your last breath.

Every time I talk or pray to God, two words from the time Dad took his last breath keeps coming to mind. Transitioning and process.

Transitioning and process. Over and over again I have never used these words before in this context. I know what this means maybe? Is Dad in between for some reason, and hasn't crossed completely over yet?

08 November - Thursday

I woke up to a quiet house. I feel so alone. I cry for Dad nonstop. I am so happy he is no longer suffering, but I miss him so deeply. I feel so empty inside. I feel the depression coming on. I feel no purpose in life except for Mom. I will stay strong for Mom.

Mom and I headed over to the mortuary to sign the final papers. We entered the parking lot of the mortuary and the only other car there was the white van that picked up Dads body the day that he passed. I walked inside and was greeted by the owner. All of a sudden I asked, "Is Dad here, is he ok, is he comfortable?" I know this might have sounded weird to them, but that is all I could think of when I walked in there. I want Dad back so bad. I cannot believe how empty I feel. I felt even worse when we left the mortuary. I felt like I was leaving him behind.

Mom and I haven't eaten for two days now. I took Mom to the place that Dad, Mom and I have gone to for 20 plus years. They know us so well there that we do not even need menus. Mom and I walked in, sat down, and right away like usual the waiter came to us. What I didn't expect brought me to tears. The waiter put down that third glass of ice water with lemon and turned to me and asked if Dad was coming. My hands went to my mouth and I started to cry uncontrollably. I couldn't believe that just those few words affected me the way they did.

When Mom and I were in the car today, I heard one of me and dad's favorite songs "I Can See Clearly Now", sung by Johnny Nash. All I could do was silently cry so Mom wouldn't hear me as I sang the words inside my head.

09 November - Friday

Another day is here and I am still breathing. I still can't believe Dad is not here. I really don't want to go on. I just want to go to sleep and never wake up. If it wasn't for Mom and my faith that God decides when, I would not be here. I would have taken my last breath with Dad.

I know he is close, because there is so much activity in the house. I feel him and so does Mom. I would love to see you, Dad. I need to know you are ok. Grandma came to me for 15 years until I spoke to her and told her I forgive her. I never saw Grandma again after that night. I believe there is an in between. Not for everyone, because I believe many pass over right away, but I do believe in others for some reason are somewhere in between.

10 November - Saturday

I am so tired. Mom is getting more depressed. She doesn't want to take her medications and wants to stay in bed. I had to get her up. I cannot let her get too deep, she needs to grieve but not give up. Mom and I went for a ride, got her favorite food, and talked. I was staying strong for her, but inside I feel numb to everything.

11 November - Sunday

I woke up to Dad's voice, so strong, right outside my door calling my name. He is closer, I feel him. I know he will come to me.

I hate the house only because Dad is not here with us. I wish he could be here with us. I wear his PJ's, T-shirts, watch, and the scapular that he wore until he took his last breath.

I wear his jacket with the Old Spice cologne scent he used to wear. I feel comfort wearing these items that he once wore himself. I love smelling his scent. I lie on his bed and sleep in it some nights; but not every night because I need to be close to Mom just in case she needs me. I feel stronger after hearing Dad, and this gives me great comfort. It gives me hope. I spoke out loud to Dad and said "I love you so much, Dad. I am taking care of Mom and I will not let her waste her life in bed. I know you would want me to take her to the beach every Sunday and out every morning to the park to walk. I love you Dad, I wish so badly that you were here." I know death is a part of life, but to lose someone after you put your life aside for almost 6 years for them is unbearable. When I am driving, I can still see Dad in the front passenger seat, looking at me and smiling like he used to.

12 November - Monday

I felt so numb and empty today. I am going to make this a good day for Mom. We went for a drive to pass time. I cannot taste my food. I can only eat once a day. I am trying, but this is so hard to accept. I remember Dad's suffering and I tell myself and to Mom that he would have never been able to live a happy, functioning life. I just wish I could be with him. This is so hard.

13 November - Tuesday

It was a very busy day today. I need to stay busy. Once I stop, all of the depressing feelings come flooding back. We went to the mortuary to drop off the urn. I asked again if Dad was here. They told me yes. I had the urge to run in there and hold him just once more. I kept picturing him on that metal bed and wondering if he was cold. I wanted to put a blanket on him. I know he's gone, but that is what I thought when I was in there. It is weird how the mind thinks of a loved one when they are gone. I wanted to kiss him. They haven't cremated him yet. I just wish that he could get up and everything be the way it was when he was healthy. They handed his clothes to me. Man, they were so cold and smelled lightly of chemicals. I held them close to my body to warm them.

14 November - Wednesday

I can't believe that it has already been a week since Dad has passed. Today is Wednesday, the day of the week he passed away, and he showed me once again that he is still around. I woke up to the scent of Old Spice cologne and the distinct smell of roses behind it. The smell of old spice is so strong.

It lasted just for a moment but long enough to bring me strength. Dad is still comforting me from the other side. He keeps me strong and I continue to believe that everything is going to be ok. Today his spiritual presence gave me great hope and happiness, and let me know that he is with me in spirit. His passing is finally hitting Mom hard. She continues to have a loss of appetite. She doesn't want to do anything but sleep and cry. I am going to give her space and let her grieve properly.

15 November - Thursday

Dad woke me up this morning. The feeling of his presence was so deep. I did not see him, but I felt him in my heart and my whole body. I couldn't see him, but it felt like he was literally inside of me. And I heard his words so clearly, as if he was right there in front of me. This is the best way I can explain how it felt with his spiritual presence. I sat up when I heard his words. Dad said, "Get up, start where we left off. I am not suffering anymore. I am happy. I love you. Tell Mom I love her. Live life and be happy, for one day we will be with each other again." I ran to Mom's room and told her what had happened and what Dad had said.

Mom felt some relief with his words, but you can tell she was hurting so bad. I have never seen her look this bad. I look into her eyes, and it brings me such pain. She looks so lost and scared. I try to comfort her but I don't think it is working. I feel so alone in this house, especially when she sleeps.

16 November - Friday

I found Mom crying again. I just want to hold her, but I know she needs to go through this to get through it. I cried so hard last night and my eyes are so swollen. There are times when I feel I am so numb, and other times I feel I cannot take anymore. I seriously have to put aside my own grief and sadness. It hurts so bad to hear Mom cry like this. She doesn't want to do anything. The hardest thing is that I cannot fix Mom's pain. In time we will be happy again. I promise you, Mom.

17 November - Saturday

It seems days and nights are flying by. What a waste. I went outside today and kept myself busy while Mom cried inside. I trimmed the roses and raked the leaves. I try to comfort Mom, but I know that what hurts the most is that Dad, the one person in our life who loved us so much and gave us so much happiness, is physically gone from our lives. It was just the 3 of us for almost 6 years. Dad, I know you know just how much you are missed, that is why you comfort Mom and I the way you do. Without you and God, I would never be able to stay this strong for Mom, let alone myself. I know we will be together one day, and I can't wait for that day.

Mom woke up tonight at 8:00. I let her sleep as long as she needed, 6 hours straight to be exact. She looks so much better. She sat down in the recliner. I made her one of her favorite meals, spaghetti and meat sauce and garlic bread with a glass of cold wine. I put on the movie "The Help" and we ate in silence. Mom laughed when it was funny, especially when it got to the part of the chocolate pie. She said "how sad" when something sad had happened. When she was done eating, she said to me, "Dad called my name." I looked at her and I saw the hope and strength this gave her in her eyes as she smiled. I said, "That's really good, Mom, I am so happy he came to you. You know he loves you so much." Mom shook her head yes with tears in her eyes. I got up and got her a glass of cold milk and made her gingerbread cookies with sprinkled sugar...she ate them all.

18 November - Saturday

I went into Mom's room when I heard her wake up. I asked her if she heard Buddy (our little Terrier) bark and jump off the bed. She told me, "Yes, I thought that was so weird and then I saw him standing down the hallway wagging his tail, What made him bark and jump off of the bed?" I told her that it was Dad and I told her what happened.

Early this morning a little after 3:00, Buddy started barking. Even though I could not see Dad, I knew he was there. I was lying on my stomach and I looked over at Buddy to the right of me. He was looking down the hallway and wagging his tail. Buddy jumped off the bed, ran to the end of the hallway and stopped abruptly. He looked up for a few seconds then cocked his head to the left side like he was listening to someone talking. He then looked back at me, looked back up, wagged his tail one last time and then came running back and jumped on my bed and licked my face. I stared down the hallway and said out loud, "I feel you here, Dad! I love you and miss you so much! Thank you for letting me know you are around every day and thank you for the kiss that Buddy gave me from you!"

19 November - Sunday

Mom came to me this morning and she said that she woke up to go to the bathroom a little after 3:00 this morning. I could tell she was upset by the way her voice sounded. She said she looked over at her dresser and Dad was right there standing next to it. He was in solid form wearing black pants and a gray t-shirt. He just stared at Mom with a solemn expression on his face. She told him to please go away because she felt scared and didn't know how to react to seeing him; especially since he had passed away in front of her. I asked Mom how Dad looked. She said he looked so healthy and younger, like when he was in his 60's. Mom said she once again told him to go away as she lay in her bed facing the wall with her back to him. She heard him moving around for a while longer and then heard him walk away out of her room. When she turned toward the hallway, it was empty.

22 November - Wednesday

Early this morning I woke up to Dad calling my name again. I looked down the hallway and saw a very large oval orb, hovering in midair in the middle of the hallway. It was shimmering with amazing color of mostly pinks and small specks of yellows and blues. It looked like a huge smooth diamond and in the middle of this orb there was a very warm white-yellow light swirling around inside. I felt such peace looking at this amazing beautiful and radiant object. I said "I love you Dad", it then disappeared.

24 November -Friday

We picked up Dad's ashes yesterday. It felt so weird holding a box with Dad's remains in them. It was so heavy. As I looked at the urn all I could think was; Dad is inside this small box. His whole body is inside this box. There are so many emotions. I still can't believe he is gone. We still hear him around us; it has become the norm. Every day we see or hear him in some way.

25 November -Saturday

At 3:27 this morning, I woke up to Dad calling my name. As I look back, I thought that it was so weird that when I heard him calling my name I just got up and went right to his room like I did when he was here physically.

I stood in his doorway with the hall light on, and I saw him sitting on his bed. He was not in solid form like he was with Mom, but transparent. He stood up when he saw me at the door. He was looking at me and moving his hands like he was in conversation, trying to tell me something. He reached out his arms to hold me as he walked toward me, I backed up when he did this because I knew I couldn't hold him the way he wanted to hold me; I knew that I would not be able to feel him in solid form.

I wished I could have held him and kissed him. I told him I loved him and I really wished I could be with him. I told Dad wherever he is; Mom and I feel him around every day. I say good morning every morning and goodnight every night to him, just as I did when he was physically here.

01 December - Friday

Last night I had a dream. This dream was different. It felt so real. I was standing in a beautiful field of endless bright flowers of every kind. The sky was a beautiful blue. The sun had such a warm beautiful glow. Out of nowhere many people appeared. They were all smiling at me. We were all wearing long white gowns. Suddenly they looked away from me and looked at something or someone coming. They all moved back and parted to give way to what was coming. I looked to see what or who was coming, and for some reason I felt so much joy for whatever it was that was making the crowd part. It was Dad. I looked into his eyes, so blue and radiant, and his smile was so big. He looked so healthy and strong with his beautiful black hair and his smooth skin. He put his arms out to me and I ran so fast yelling, "Dad!" When I reached him I held onto him so tight; and he hugged me tight back. I was so happy and I felt so much peace being there with him. No more emptiness, no more sadness, just peace and so much happiness. I then woke up flooded with such sadness; I did not want to wake up from this beautiful dream.

Mom and I have been keeping busy. We still comment on how we still can't believe Dad is physically gone. Mom and I feel a difference in the house the past few days. We know Dad will always be with us in spirit, but the energy level, the feeling of his deep presence, is almost non-existent. I still feel Dad around, but Mom and I think maybe he crossed over.

This morning I woke up early. I thought I would surprise Mom with a Christmas tree. I always see Dad in my mind and feel his presence in the car. He gave me so many laughs and good memories of singing songs together in the car. I still see his beautiful blue eyes looking at me in the front seat of the car. He used to just stare and smile at me and when I looked over, he would always wink and give me a big smile and say, "I love you".

First, I took Buddy to the park then the lake. I shed some tears because I miss Dad being with me so bad. The lake was one of our favorite spots. I stood at the water's edge and I told Dad I miss him and I wish he was here. I told him that I am holding strong because I know one day I will be with him again. Every time that I go to the places that we went on a daily basis, I am now going to them alone. This is so hard to do. I feel so empty coming here without him.

After the lake I headed over to the tree farm. Dad always said, "Not too big, not to small." So I picked a tree that he would have picked; 6.5 feet and flocked white. This tree was so perfect. I brought the tree home and brought it inside. I loved the smile Mom gave me. She loved it. This year will be the first year without Dad being here physically, but I know he will see all of the extra lights and decorations that I am putting up for him and Mom this year.

10 December - Sunday

Something happened last night as I slept in Dad's bed. All I can remember is Buddy's heart beating fast and moving around on the bed. No matter what I did, I couldn't fully wake up to see what it was. But I knew something was happening, something was there.

I woke up this morning and looked over where Dad's closet is. His closet doors are about 8 feet tall with mirrors on them. For just a moment I saw Dad in the mirror. He was at the foot of the bed looking down at me. He looked very healthy. His hair was darker and he was wearing a green and white plaid print long sleeve shirt with black pants. His arms were down in front of him with his hands clasped together, and his head was tilted to the left. He had a smile on his face when he was looking at me. He had a look of deep love and admiration.

I was so happy to know he is still around. When I tell people that Dad comes to Mom and me in some way on a daily basis, they say they have heard that loved ones come and nurture us for some time after their passing. Grandma visited me for 15 years, and before the night of Grandma's last visit, she came to me almost on a monthly basis.

I truly believe that not one faith knows all of the answers to why things happen the way they do, or if they really happen. I believe in the Bible and I also know that there are too many unexplained things that are not mentioned in the bible. Really everyone has a different answer. For me I know what is true and that is all that matters. I do have questions of things that have happened in my life, and what I have personally witnessed for myself. I believe that when the time comes, we will have all of our questions answered; and it won't be by anyone here on earth.

12 December - Wednesday

Today was Dad's funeral. I did not want to go. Too many emotions. Too many things going on. Now that it is all said and done, I am just happy today is over with. So many good people showed up to support me and Mom. I just feel so empty without Dad. I still can't believe he is gone. I am trying to move on. I know everyone has their time to leave this world. But I just feel so empty without Dad.

I did not like the dream I had last night. A little before Dad passed, I had to clear mucus from his airway. No matter how much I tried to get it all out, it kept coming up again. About an hour before he passed, he tried so desperately to tell me something, but his voice was only a whisper and I couldn't understand. Because of the fluids in his throat, his voice was too low for me to hear what he was trying to say.

In my dream, really a nightmare, Dad was laying in his bed. His mouth was open and he was trying to say something to me. I looked into his mouth and his mouth kept filling up with blood. I tried over and over to take it out, but as the dream was going on, it filled up faster and faster. No matter what I did, and no matter how I tried to take it out, it filled up faster and faster. As I did this, Dad was trying to tell me something. I was desperately trying to save him because I needed to hear what he was trying to tell me. I felt so scared and desperate in this dream. I needed to hear what he was saying, but I never did get to hear what he said to me. When I woke up crying, I heard clear as day in Dad's voice, "Patreesha!". I said out loud, "Dad I miss you so much!"

16 December -Sunday

I slept in Dads bed again last night. About 5:00 this morning, I first felt the bed bump like someone does when they try and wake you up. My eyes snapped open and I waited. Again I felt Dad's bed being bumped.

I laid there listening and thinking "did I really feel the bed being bumped?" I heard something small tapping or hitting something solid nearby. I looked for where the tapping was coming from. My eyes started to focus on Dad's medal of St. Anthony hanging from the bed post. It was slowly swinging back and forth and hitting the bed post to the left of me. I laid there on my stomach just watching it going back and forth. I looked around. The fan wasn't on and no windows were open. I thought it was so odd that the chain was swinging in a smooth movement back and forth, even after it hit the bed post. Wouldn't it bounce before swinging again? I slowly reached for the medal as it was swinging in midair and held it in my hand for about two seconds. When I gently let go, again the medal pulled back in midair and started moving back and forth on its own, tapping the bedpost. I felt such great joy. I knew it was Dad. I told him that I missed him and I loved him and thanked him for coming once again to comfort me. After saying those words out loud to Dad, the chain stopped moving.

07 November 2013

One year to the day after Dad's passing, Dad appeared to me in solid form. I woke up lying on my stomach and slowly lifted my head. I felt something different around me. I looked to my left and saw Dad lying next to me. He was peacefully sleeping, letting me know that even when I sleep, he is always with me. The moment I closed my eyes for just a second, he was gone.

02 February 2014

Today is Dad's Birthday and once again Dad made his presence known today. Mom and I were watching T.V. and all of a sudden Buddy jumped off Mom's lap and sat on the floor facing her. He had such an intense look on his face looking at her. I watched him for some time and then noticed that he was not watching her, but staring above her head. Mom said that she felt uncomfortable not only by how he was staring at her, but how long he stared at her. I looked over to where Mom was sitting and saw what Buddy was staring at. Dad was wearing his favorite light blue sweatshirt and he looked like he did at 83 but when he was healthy looking. He stood behind Mom in her recliner. He had each of his hands resting on the chair to each side of her head, smiling at me...

For just a moment he showed himself, and then disappeared.

Dad has appeared to Mom and me periodically since he has passed. I have the feeling that he will continue to visit us until we are called home.

Dad's Message

23 December 2012

Last night I cried so hard. The weight of guilt on my shoulders is so heavy. Every minute of every day since Dad's passing, I think of how he suffered every day for so long. Maybe he wouldn't have suffered so much if I could have done it this way or that way. Maybe if I tried this type of therapy, or taken him to this type of doctor, or if I had done a certain type of therapy longer, then just maybe he wouldn't have suffered so much. Or maybe he could have been cured if I would have just tried one more thing.

I also felt guilt for the night before he passed, that I should have laid with him all night instead of the few hours that I did, even though I could not take the endless sounds of his lungs filling up and his breathing stopping every few minutes. Even though I laid with him that night for some time, I just couldn't handle the whole night. Mentally and physically I was drained from being up four days straight, massaging Dad's body and turning him every 2 hours to make sure his body didn't stiffen up or develop any bed sores. But still after all that reasoning with myself, I felt so guilty.

All I know is that all of this, all of these years, took a toll on me, and Mom, too. Now we feel so lost and alone without Dad.

I couldn't get the night before Dad's passing out of my mind. How I was laying there next to him on the couch listening to him sigh so loud, taking deep breaths in and then loudly sighing. To this day his loud sighs haunt my memory. Here I worked with 911 for almost 17 years, and I couldn't even call them to help Dad. I had to lay there and not do anything but tell him he was not alone, periodically caress his hair, hold his hand, and massage him.

I wanted to scream and beg for God to please make this stop. Make these thoughts stop. I can't take it anymore. I couldn't save him, I couldn't help him. I had to lay there and listen to him slowly die. This ate at me every day since he had passed. Mentally my mind was slowly breaking me. So I spoke with God out loud because I really couldn't take anymore. I said, "God please take this weight off my shoulders, take this guilt from my mind, and bring me mental peace! Please either You or Dad come to me. I need to hear from one of you that I did everything possible. Because I can't take it anymore!" I finally cried myself to sleep.

Early the next morning I woke up and looked down the hallway. What I saw was amazing. The living room was no longer the living room, it was another dimension. Or Heaven?

The first thing that I noticed was how I personally felt. I felt only two things, peace and happiness. This inner peaceful warmth filled every cell in my body. The sun was very bright, but very different from here on earth. It was a beautiful bright yellow-white light, but the brightness did not affect my eyes in any way. My mind was completely empty of any earthly thoughts or feelings. I felt no depression, no sadness, no anger or resentment, just deep peace and happiness beyond anything I have ever felt. The second thing I noticed was the lush green rolling hills and bright deep blue skies. No clouds, no cars or buildings. I saw so many people. I heard them laughing. And then beyond them, I saw Dad. He was surrounded by so many children, laughing and playing. He was illuminated with this beautiful yellow-white light, even brighter than the sun shining around him. He stood there so proud with his hands clasped in front of him, staring at me with this proud smile on his face saying to me "I made it!" He wore a long sleeve, thin blue striped white dress shirt with light blue pants.

Besides what Dad had said to me, there is one thing I will never forget, and that was his eyes. I have never seen this in anyone ever. Once again even his eyes were brighter than himself and illuminated with that soft radiant yellow-white light; like 3D. Even though he was about 30 feet away from me, it was as if his eyes were right in front of mine. They were the most beautiful piercing blue, like crystal clear water. They were so perfect, like smooth diamonds. I saw Buddy run to Dad, and Dad bent down to pet Buddy and said, "Hi Bubba, hi Bubba, how's my Bubba!?" Just like he did when he was here on earth.

I cried out, "Dad, Dad, Dad!" I stood up from my bed and I went to run to him, but a man's gentle voice to the right of me said, "No, you cannot go where he is right now. It is not your time yet, you cannot go into the light." I sat back down on my bed and I started to cry because I wanted to be with him. I needed to hold him. I cried out to Dad again and then he stood up, smiled at me, looked me right in my eyes, and spoke with a gentle, peaceful voice. He said, "It's ok...It's ok...don't worry...When it is your time. When it is meant to be, I will be waiting at the door for you." He then disappeared.

What I had just witnessed was amazing. Dad looked beautiful. I sat on my bed and thought how peaceful it felt there. No thoughts of worry, anxiety or sadness; nothing but deep peace and happiness. I will remember forever the hope that I was given to stay strong till it is my time. I am content knowing Dad is truly happy and no longer suffering. That he is where he deserves to be, living in the eternal peace and happiness he never experienced in his life on earth. I feel so much joy right now. I keep telling Mom over and over what happened, and each time I cannot find the perfect words to explain just how beautiful the other side is. There are no human words to explain just how beautiful and peaceful it is on the other side.

I Remember When

The last five years and five months of Dad's life and his journey with Alzheimer's brought Mom and me so many precious moments. Even though our journey with Dad was very hard and at times depressing, the moments of laughter and love kept all three of us going. These were just some of the most memorable moments of my life with this man I will always cherish and hold onto forever:

I remember when one Christmas in 1974; Dad had six dollars left in his pocket. He went out and bought us six kids each a present for a dollar. He bought me a red vinyl purse with a black cat on it. I was so proud of this purse. The first thing I did was open the purse and smell it. (For some reason I always smelled my gifts. Why, I do not know.)

I remember when, on the night of Christmas Eve in 1975, the doorbell rang. We all looked at each other because it was late at night and we were getting ready for bed. Mom yelled out, "I wonder who that could be!" She opened the front door and there was a big red plastic bag sitting in front of the open doorway. She picked up the big red bag and brought it in and opened it and said, "Looks like Santa was here!" We watched Mom take each wrapped present and put them under the tree. This happened four times that night. Each time, Mom would say and do the same thing. After the fourth doorbell ring, I finally discovered who was putting those big red bags full of presents outside the front door. I saw Dad dressed in a Santa suit run by the back glass door with a red bag over his shoulder. I don't think he noticed that the white beard was hanging from his face as we made eye contact. I said, "Hey Mom, I just saw Dad dressed as Santa, run by the back door!" Mom told me, "No, your Dad is at work. It's not him." I knew what I saw, and it was definitely Dad dressed as Santa.

I remember when it was my 7th birthday; Dad took me to Toys R Us. He held my hand as he walked toward the entrance of the store. I looked up at him and said, "Dad we're at Toys R Us. Why are we here?"

He looked down at me with a smile on his face. We stopped just inside the entrance and he said to me, "You can pick one thing for your birthday. Anything you want in this store you can have." I said, "I can have anything I want!?" Dad said, "Yes one thing, anything you want." I was so happy but shocked at the same time. He told me to take my time looking. Our childhood did not consist of getting lots of gifts, especially expensive gifts. Being here at Toys R Us was overwhelming, but exciting at the same time. I walked up and down each aisle as Dad held my hand, looking at dolls, bikes and games. Then we came to the Barbie aisle and I saw what I wanted. The 1976 Barbie star traveler motorhome. I was on top of the world. Dad kept asking me, "Are you sure this is what you want?" And I replied, "Yes, yes, yes, this is what I want!" It wasn't just the gift that Dad bought me; it was Dad holding my hand. I always cherished that rare moment with my Dad because he rarely gave that type of attention.

 I remember when in 1977 Dad took us out to eat at an Italian restaurant. We were seated at a booth, and we were each handed a menu. I noticed Dad looking at Mom and saying, "We can't do it." Mom said, "What do you mean?" Dad said," I don't have enough, it's too expensive. We can't eat here." Dad looked at us and said, "Sorry, but we can't eat here. How about some hot chocolate?" He ordered eight hot chocolates. When the hot chocolates were put in front of us, each one had marshmallows in them. The nice waiter knew that Dad did not have money for dinner, so he tried to lighten the mood by setting crayons and coloring paper in front of us with our hot chocolates. The waiter said, "How about that, guys!? How does that taste!? Good!?" All I remember is the six of us children saying, "This is so good" or "yum" and "thanks Dad" after each sip. We were humbled children at that time. We were nowhere near living in luxury, so the hot chocolate we had that day really did make us happy.

 I remember when Dad took us on vacations each summer from 1981 to 1983. He took us to see all of the historical sites across the U.S. My favorite places were the Grand Canyon, Mount Rushmore, Yellowstone Park (minus the smell) and Niagara Falls. Dad bought us fishing poles, a knife to cut the fish, and mess kits to put our food on. He not only taught us how to fish, but he taught us how to hike and what dangers to look out for when hiking on the trails. One of the most memorable moments of our vacation in 1983 was when we went to visit Mrs. Ovitt, the lady that took Dad in at 12 years old. Barbara Ovitt was such a beautiful and compassionate lady. Before we got to the farm in Vermont, we set up our camp site before we headed back. On the way back to the farm, we passed an ice cream stand where they made huge ice cream cones with vanilla ice cream with hot fudge on the bottom and the top of the cone. Dad bought us one each and we ate them on the way to the farm. Mrs. Ovitt showed us the farm Dad worked on, the fields where he plowed the soil, and the room where he slept. The Ovitt's left Dad's room exactly the way he left it in 1948. Here it was 1983, 35 years later, still in the same condition. After visiting Mrs. Ovitt, we passed by the ice cream stand again and Dad asked us if we wanted another one; and of course we would all yell "Yeah!" We passed by that ice cream stand two more times before we left town the next day.

I remember when I got into a couple of fights in school. One particular fight, Dad was home. I was sitting in the principal's office dreading his arrival to come sign me out and take me home. I remember the door swinging open and the sun brightly shining in as I saw the silhouette of dad walking through the door. I gulped hard. I thought; man, am I in so much trouble. Dad said "Did you win the fight?" I weakly answered "Yes". Dad said "Good, let's get you signed out and get the hell out of here". Dad gave me a talk on the way home. I remember him telling me "You never start or look for a fight, but when you get in one you better make sure you end it". Dad also said "Just remember, there will always be someone bigger, better, stronger and tougher than you".

I remember when in 1989 when Dad bought me my first car. It was a 1989 white Dodge Omni Hatchback. I remember coming home and walking up the driveway, Dad was standing there next to the car with a smile on his face holding out the keys to me. I stood there and just looked at Dad and then back to my new car. I said, "That's my car Dad!?" and he said, "Yep, but with three conditions. No drinking and driving, always wear your seat belt and....No boys in the car. Ok, you promise?" I said, "I promise!" I kept every promise except the boy promise.

I remember when Dad, Mom and I would go to the lake and beach every day. I remember when not a day would go by that Dad and I were not together 24/7. I remember how Dad and I would go to the movies two times a week, and always the night before I would go to him and say, "Tomorrow is movie day!" and he would say, "It is!? Oh boy! Tomorrow is going to be a good day!"

I remember when Dad was forgetting how to spell simple words. I started finding sticky notes in his room, his bathroom and his computer room and they had one word written on every single one of them "Jeezus". I gathered everyone one of them and put them in the zip lock baggy that holds every movie we ever went to from 2007 to 2012 along with every note he ever wrote me that he would slip them periodically under my door to either tell me he loves me or the boogey man is in town and to beware. I laugh and cry each time I look at them. I find at times that I need to touch what he once touched and reconnect with these memories to bring me strength. I was blessed to have countless moments with my Dad that I will cherish forever.

I remember when Dad would make me laugh in the store when he would hear music, especially 50's music, and he would dance for me or anyone who would take interest. He loved to dance and he loved to make people laugh.

I remember when as time went on, Dad would shake his head and say that he couldn't stand that he couldn't remember. So I would purposely say I couldn't remember something and he would get so happy. I would tell him, "See Dad, you're not the only one who forgets." And he would say, "Good. I am so happy I am not the only one who forgets."

I remember when Dad would come to my bedroom multiple times every night asking me if he kissed me good night yet because he would forget just 5 minutes earlier that he already kissed me goodnight. I would always tell him each time "No", so he wouldn't feel bad. He would come over to me and kiss me on my forehead and ask me, "Same ole same ole, nothing new for tomorrow?" I would always respond, "Same ole same ole, nothing new, maybe a movie." I remember after Dad kissing me good night, he would reach over and play, "This little piggy went to market" with my toes, and how we would both laugh. The first time he forgot to come to my room for our nightly routine, I cried because it was such a special thing we did every night without fail.

I remember when he would always yell out "Yee haw!" after every joke. When he would pass gas and look down at the ground and say, "Look at the mouse!" Or he would look up at the sky or ceiling and say, "What the hell was that!?"

I remember when each time we would pass the bakery; Dad would look at me like a little boy and say "Can I have one?" I would tell him of course, and he would always get two donuts, a glazed twist and an old fashioned chocolate.

I remember when we would go to the movies and Dad would always ask for Reece's peanut butter cups, buttered popcorn, and water. I also remember when he would want to leave just 30 minutes into the movie because his anxiety was starting up. Three of the last movies that we saw were the Disney movies Brave, Puss and Boots, and Toy Story 3.

I remember when Dad could only use a certain fork or spoon or cup. And he could only wear certain tops, always with a pocket. I remember he could only have two to three objects of food on his plate in small portions. If not, he would just shut down and not eat.

I remember when we would go for a drive and he would just sit in the passenger front seat and stare at me, and when I would look over and say, "Dad what are you staring at!?" he would wink and point at me and say, " You. I love you."

I remember when he and I were listening to the song in the car by Rod Stewart called "Have I Told You Lately," and Dad interrupted me and said "Shhh! This song right here, I dedicate this song to you and I mean every word of it." Then he said to me, "I dedicate this song to Mom too. You both mean everything to me. You are both my best friends."

I remember when he could no longer dress himself, and I would dress him. I told him not to worry, that everyone needs help sometime in their life. He would smile and say, "I'm just glad I have you."

I remember when listening to the music in the car, Dad would always slap his right hand on his right knee in time with the music. I especially remember the Johnny Cash songs. Dad would copy the sounds of each singer whether they were a deep man's voice or a woman's voice and we both would laugh so hard.

I remember when going to eat breakfast with Mom and Dad a few times a week, and Dad would always ask the same question because he couldn't read the menu anymore. He would ask, "What are you going to eat?" I told him we would have the same thing, two eggs, wheat toast, and hash browns; because his Alzheimer's mind could no longer make choices, let alone read what was on the menu. He would get so happy because I would order for him, because he didn't want the waitress to know that he couldn't read from the menu anymore.

I remember when the time came that he could no longer tie his shoes; I would tie them for him. And then so we could have him continue to work his mind, we got Velcro shoes for him. Then the day came when he couldn't put those on and I would do it for him, and he would shake his head in shame. I would tell him, "It's ok Dad. I do not mind doing it." I told him that I have trouble with my shoes too, and he would say "Really!?" and I told him yes, and he would say, "Good, I'm glad I'm not the only one!"

I remember when Dad would love to play multiple finger and hand games with me as we waited for our food to be served to us. One of them was the dismember finger trick and Dad would say to me "Look I have no thumb!" and he would laugh like it was the first time telling the joke each time. He would also like to play slaps or one of Dad's favorites, thumb wrestling. Dad would also love to play which hand is it in, or his all-time favorite steeple people. I remember as his Alzheimer's progressed, he would forget how to do each one. It was so devastating to me each time he forgot each one till one day he forgot how to do all of them.

I remember when I would put him to sleep and I would walk away to leave his room and hear him do the "Charge" horn sound with his mouth. I would almost fall to the ground with laughter each time he would do this.

I remember when some people told me that there would be a day that I would have to put him in a home. I told each of them that I would die before that happens. I was so happy that God gave me the strength and compassion to take care of him till the end. It was a privilege to take care of Dad. He brought so much joy not only to me, but Mom, and anyone who took the time out of their life to be in his presence.

I remember when I asked him if he feared dying. He would say, "Hell no, when it is my time to go I am ready to go! I know I will go to a good place! I just want to make sure you and Mom will be ok." He then said to me while pointing at me, "You know you could go before me." He laughed at me and said, "Now... How scared are you? Yee haw!" We both laughed.

I remember when in the summer of 2011, I took Dad to the lake and we talked for a while. I asked if he had one wish, what it would be. He said he has everything, so he would wish for me to have everything I need.I asked him the same questions every day. I'll never forget the day I asked; "Dad, who am I to you?" He looked at me and stopped walking. Tears filled his eyes as he stared at me and said, "I don't know who you are to me, I am sorry. I mean, I know you mean something to me, but I don't know who you are." I told him its ok, I am your daughter. He looked at me and said, "You're my daughter!? I thought you were my son! Yee haw! " I laughed because it really was funny, but I was also glad that I was wearing my sunglasses to hide the tears.

I remember when I spoke with Dad because I had been noticing he had been changing his underwear a lot, and he had been leaving "little gifts" in his underwear. So I went in his room and closed the door. I asked him if he was starting to lose control of his bowels. I let him know that it happens to a lot of people. He didn't answer me, so I asked him if he is pooping or peeing in his pants. He said, "No are you!?" I laughed and asked, "Then what is that?" as I pointed down to his underwear that lay on the floor at his ankles. He took a pause, slowly looked down, and then slowly looked up. He whispered, "It's candy, you want some?" I laughed so hard and said, "No! That is not candy, Dad!" I got up and said, "Forget it." I kissed him goodnight and left it alone for another day.

I remember when I drove him to get his mail, paper, and lunch before I went back out to run a personal errand. I dropped him off and opened the gate. He just stood there looking at me as I was locking the gate. I looked into his eyes to say I would be back, but he had tears in his eyes. He said, "Please be careful and come back safe, I need you." I said, "Okay, I will be back safe. I love you and I will be back soon." He just stood there and looked at me. So I said, "Dad it's hot out, please go inside. If you don't go now, I am going to put you on restriction!" He said "Yippy!" and ran back to the house. I watched him close the screen door to the porch, stand there and continue to watch me leave.

I remember when I came back from a doctor's appointment Dad greeted me at the door with tears in his eyes. He said, "You made it home! I am the happiest man in the world!" I always cherished those times when he would greet me at the door, especially the last time just days before he took his last breath.

I remember when I took Mom and Dad shoe shopping. Dad was so excited to get new shoes. He got a new pair of white Nikes with blue trim (they are still in the same place in the bathroom under the table where he told me to hide them just days before he passed). I had to laugh. They looked like little kids wearing brand new shoes. Dad was so proud of his shoes, he kept saying, "I love my new shoes so much. Don't you like my new shoes!?" The rest of the day we went to the post office, the grocery store, etc. Every person that Dad would pass, he would tell them to look at his new shoes and ask them if they liked them. We laughed a lot that day.

I remember when in August of 2010, Dad came to me and told me he wants to give up, that he doesn't want to do anything anymore. I wanted to cry, but I thought, no way. Mom and I will not let him give up. I told Dad it was ok to get down, we all do. But to give up, I would not let him, because he still had so much life left in him. I made a plan to take him outside and keep his mind busy. I wanted him to feel useful, like he was still a productive part of life. I made sure when we were trimming the trees that I would cut the branch till it was about to break, and then hand him the saw and have him cut the rest till it completely broke off, making it look like he did it. It worked! He felt so proud and his mood was so much stronger after that. Every day after that I made a point to involve Dad in something that made him feel alive and strong, and to make decisions that made him feel that he was in control of himself.

I remember when Dad's doctor visits were some of the funniest moments we had together. The doctor would come in and ask how Dad is doing. Dad would start by saying "My rectum is good! How is yours doing?" I would laugh so hard and so did the doctor. It went downhill from there.

I remember when Mom, Dad and I went outside to plant some more trees. As always, Dad was eager to help, but it never lasted long. So here I was digging holes, and Mom held the hose to soften the dirt, and Dad had the fertilizer. We got done with a tree and I noticed Dad was not with us anymore. Mom and I looked around and we noticed him heading for the house. I said, "Hey Dad, where are you going!?" He continued to walk away with his back to us with his hand waving in the air and saying, "I am going to take a shower. I worked really hard today and I am going to lay down for a nap too!" Mom and I looked at each other and laughed. Mom said, "Ok George, take it easy."

I remember when Dad and I decided to go see Toy Story 3. In between scenes, I would look over and watch Dad's face. He smiled and laughed the whole time. He could not take his eyes off the screen, not once. As we walked out, I asked him how he liked the movie. He said "What movie, we saw a movie!?" I smiled at him but I was crying inside, and I said, "Come on Dad, it's time to go home." I thought to myself, at least he enjoyed the moment when he was watching the movie.

I remember when we were kids and movie rentals just came out in our town. Dad would rent about 10 VHS movies to watch on the weekends after doing our chores. We would watch movies all day long. He would order pizza and soda and after eating he would always go to the kitchen and do the same routine. We would hear the cupboards open and glass dishes being taken out. Dad would set each glass bowl next to each other in a row, stop and look at us and continue to take pleasure in us watching with anticipation for us to get some candy. Dad would always stand in front of the counter facing us to make sure we could hear and see him. He would then hold up bags of candy and just stare at us with a "Jack Nicholson" look on his face and we would laugh. Dad would then slowly open each bag and stare at us as we intently stared back at him. He would open each bag and one by one drop each piece of candy into each bowl. He would wait for each candy to hit the bowl to make that "Ping" sound and then let another one fall from his fingers. In between dropping one piece at a time he would look up, smile, stare and then once again slowly continue to put each candy in each bowl. When he was done putting candy in each bowl he would yell out in a sarcastic "I want you to beg" tone of voice "Who wants candy!" And of course we would instantly yell back "I do!"

I remember when Dad came to my room one night, about 6 months before he passed away calling out my name "Patreesha!" I heard not only sadness, but fear. He sounded lost. I said "What's wrong Dad?" He said "Can you show me the path to take home, can you show me the way home to my mom? Can you help me get home?" It took everything I had in me to not cry right there. His voice, sounded so small, so scared like a child who couldn't find his mom. I said "Dad, of course I can help you. I will take you home tomorrow ok?" Dad said "You will? You'll take me to where my mom is. You'll take me home? You know the path home?" I said "Yes Dad, I know the way home, I know the path to take you home to see your mom. You better get a good night's sleep ok. You have a big day tomorrow" Dad said "Oh boy, I'm the happiest man in the world! Thank you. Thank you so much!" Dad kissed me good night and walked down the hallway toward his room, where I heard him tell Mom that I was going to take him home to his mom tomorrow. Luckily, the next morning, he forgot all about his mom.

I remember when Dad and I would have one-hour mind strengthening classes, once a day, Monday through Friday. I said, "Ok Dad, we are done for the day with class and we will continue this tomorrow." He said, "I will be playing hooky tomorrow!" I said, "Really Dad!? Why will you be playing hooky tomorrow?" He said, "I don't like the teacher; she's a bitch...Yee haw!"

I remember when lying down for a moment to relax because I just came in from watering the rose bushes in 103 degree weather. I woke up about an hour later, drenched in sweat. I checked the air condition to see if it was on, and I saw that it was over 100 degrees in the house. Dad had turned on the heater.

I remember when I walked into Dad's room 6 months before his passing, and he looked so happy. He was rubbing his hands together and saying "Yippy!" I asked him why he was so happy and he said, "I am the happiest man in the world because I am going to go see my mom soon!" I asked him if that was what his mom told him. He said,

"No, that is what I told her." I hugged him and held him and cried silently because I knew what he was saying was true. I knew his time was coming soon.

I remember when on rainy days Dad and I would walk into the stores to shop and as we went up each aisle of toys we would purposely twist our feet on the tile floor to make them squeak, then we would squeeze each toy that made sounds to turn them all on at once. We laughed so hard. All you could hear was squeaky feet and all of the toys playing some kind of music or weird noise. Some people would laugh, some would look irritated. We didn't care. We were having fun. I miss this so much.

I remember when Mom and I went to the mall (Before Dad developed Alzheimer's). As we shopped we noticed a man with a long black trench coat, black sunglasses and a hat walking behind us, hiding behind pillars and looking through the store windows as we shopped. I mentioned to Mom, do you see that man, I think he is following us. Just as Mom turned to look, security came up behind the man and started questioning him. The man took off his hat and sunglasses and pointed toward us. I said out loud "Mom, it's Dad!" I couldn't stop laughing. Long story short we explained to security that we knew him and Dad was let off with a warning.

I remember when I was shopping one time for myself and I looked up and Dad was gone. I heard in a low voice "Patreesha!" I looked and around and said out loud "Dad!" Once again I heard a faraway low voice "Patreesha!" I scanned the store and said "Dad, where are you!?" I looked around again and finally found Dad in between a clothes rack in the aisle over. Dad was peeking through the middle of the clothes. I laughed so hard. I said "Dad, get out of there, you are going to get us kicked out!" Dad yelled out "Yee haw!"

I remember when Dad and I were taking a drive in Temecula and we entered a construction zone. There was a group of construction workers standing on the corner. As we approached, Dad told me to put the window down. I already had a smile on my face because knowing Dad he was going to start some trouble. As the window went down, Dad put his hand out the window and with a feminine wave with his fingers moving back and forth yelling in a very high sweet voice "Hi boys, how ya doing cuties!"...I laughed so hard, luckily so did the construction workers.

I remember when I would give Dad his showers and I would wash his hair and face. Without fail, Dad would yell out "Holy shit! What are you trying to do rip my skin off!? I would always say back to him while trying not to laugh out loud "Dad, stop acting like a Baaaaby! And Dad would say "Stop acting like a biiiitch! We would both laugh until he decided to complain again about something else I was doing.

I remember when one day Mom, Dad and I picked up some food and headed to the lake to have a little picnic. I opened up the car door and Buddy (our terrier) jumped out. I would call for him multiple times and he would just ignore me. Dad said "He should listen to you, you are his master". So I said to Mom jokingly "I am his master and he needs to listen to me. Give me a piece of your sandwich so I can use it as bait to get him back in the car" I held out the food as I called out to Buddy. He ran back and jumped in and just as he did I heard Dad's voice from the back seat say "So I guess you are the masterrrr...baterrrr!". I choked on my tea as Mom said to Dad "George you are not supposed to speak to your daughter like that!". I was laughing so hard. I looked in the rearview mirror and I said in between laughing "Dad you are nasty, you need to stop!" Dad mouthed the same words so Mom couldn't hear and yelled out "Yee haw."

Made in the USA
San Bernardino, CA
25 September 2016